Library Media Center
Carroll Community College
1601 Washington Road
and 21157

LIBRARIE

LIBRARY PATRONS AND THE LAW

ARLENE BIELEFIELD • LAWRENCE CHEESEMAN

NEAL-SCHUMAN PUBLISHERS, INC.

NEW YORK   LONDON

"This publication is designed to provide accurate and authoritative information in regard to the subject matter covered. It is sold with the understanding that the publisher is not engaged in rendering legal, accounting or other professional service. If legal advice or other expert assistance is required, the services of a competent professional person should be sought."

From a Declaration of Principles adopted jointly by a Committee of the American Bar Association and a Committee of Publishers.

All rights reserved. Reproduction of this book in whole or in part, without written permission if the publisher, is prohibited.

Printed and bound in the United States of America

Library of Congress Cataloging-in-Publication Data

Bielefield, Arlene.
    Library patrons and the law / by Arlene Bielefield, Lawrence Cheeseman.
       p.   cm. — (Libraries & the law series)
    Includes bibliographical references (p.) and index.
    ISBN 1-55570-132-9
    1. Library legislation—United States. 2. Privacy, Right of—United States. 3. Libraries—Censorship—United States. 4. Civil rights—United States. I. Cheeseman, Lawrence. II. Title.
III. Series.
KF4315.B54   1995
344.73'092—dc20
[347.30492]   95-16178

Contents

Part III: Library Applications

Appendixes

Introduction

Over the last three years, the authors have presented a number of workshops and classes on the topic of libraries and the law. During our presentations, we became aware of the need for a series of books on the law as it relates to libraries of all types, whether public or private. The series needs to be tailored specifically for librarians, library staff members, and those who govern libraries.

This volume is part of six-book series addressing that specific need. While none of these books are intended to replace legal advice, the set is intended to help those interested in libraries to learn the basics of the law as it relates to libraries in the areas of:

- copyright,
- employment,
- contract,
- patron rights,
- library facilities, and
- library governance.

It has been our experience that once these basics are understood, there is a greater awareness that many decisions and actions taken in libraries have significant legal consequences. With that realization, those who work in and run libraries are better able to judge when they need to seek the specific advice of counsel. Too often an action is taken and professional advice is sought after the problem has occurred.

Because today's American society is actively litigious, we feel it is necessary for libraries to learn how to practice *defensive law*. Like defensive driving, this method is meant to prevent accidents—in this case, legal accidents—by anticipating a problem and taking affirmative steps to avoid it. It makes sense to foresee a legal problem before taking an action, because even winning a case is expensive and time consuming. Losing a case could mean disaster.

Since each situation is different, care must always be taken. One should never assume that an action can or cannot be taken based upon someone else's experience. The law seems at times almost incomprehensible, and the old law school admonition to "look to the language of the law" does not always make the situation clearer. Many times there are ambiguities and not even lawyers are exactly sure what a particular law means until it is tested in the courts. This can take time.

For example, take the Americans with Disabilities Act of 1990. This law ensures that citizens with disabilities may participate in public services, including access to public library facilities. There have been volumes written on this statute already. Some parts of the statute are clear. However, other parts, like the phrase "reasonable accommodation," are less than clear. Undoubtedly, more court cases will emerge to clarify what that and other phrases in the statute mean. It is our hope that these cases will not be brought against libraries, and, to that end, we have explained the law at length in the area of access to library facilities.

This book, like the rest of the series, is written for non-lawyers. Plain language is used throughout.

This book is divided into three parts. Part I deals with the constitutional rights of library patrons, including the First Amendment rights to information and to privacy. Part II deals with the statutory and other rights of patrons, including freedom of information laws, document depository systems, the Americans with Disabilities Act, library policies, and librarians' codes of ethics. Part III covers library applications, including developing library rules of conduct and dealing with censorship. Part III also includes a series of frequently asked questions from patrons about library rules and regulations. Each is followed by a suggested answer.

At the beginning of each chapter is a set of questions to help focus attention on important issues in that chapter. Appendixes include the text of an important case and a statute covered in the body of the book.

Each volume in the series stands alone and also complements the other volumes. Some topics may appear in more than one volume—for example, there is some coverage of library access by the disabled in the volume dealing with library facilities, as well as in this volume.

Each book covers its subject in a way that should be useful to all types of libraries. The volume that covers the duties and responsibilities of trustees and friends, while it has a public library emphasis, also concerns library friends groups. Friends groups may support any type of library, so even this volume, apparently focused on public libraries, can serve other types of libraries as well.

Readers of this series will find that they have a better understanding of what the law says and also what it does not say relating to everyday activities in libraries. The series will also help libraries practice defensive law and avoid legal problems before they occur.

Part I
Constitutional Rights

1

Libraries and the Courts

- *Are rules and regulations concerning use of a library absolute and above challenge in the courts?*
- *What legal developments are behind the recent changes in the court's view of library patrons' rights?*
- *How has the historic importance and the expanding role of libraries in modern society affected patrons' right of access?*
- *What role have the courts seen for libraries?*

Throughout their history, libraries have placed restrictions on the use of their facilities and collections. Among other things, these restrictions, in the form of library rules and regulations, have determined who could use the library and how patrons must behave in the library. Violation of these use regulations have resulted in patrons being expelled, having their library privileges suspended, or being banned outright from using, entering, or even contacting the library.

Until recently these library use regulations could not be challenged in the courts unless they violated a local law that governs the operation of the library. These library regulations are after all essential to:

- preserving the library's collections and facilities;
- protecting library staff and patrons; and
- maintaining an atmosphere in the library that is conducive to study and learning.

Recently, however, the courts have ruled that these use regulations are not absolute and that they can be challenged on constitutional and other grounds in the courts.

7

There are several legal developments behind this significant change in the courts' role in library affairs. Chief among these is the development in the U.S. Supreme Court of two separate but interrelated doctrines—the constitutional right to receive ideas and information (Chapter 3)[1] and the constitutional right to privacy (Chapter 5).[2] The Court has also ruled that library use regulations must be made and enforced in a reasonable manner that is equally applicable to all, and that these use regulations cannot be used as a pretext for pursuing those engaged in lawful, constitutionally protected exercise of their fundamental rights (Chapter 4).[3] Some new state and federal legislative enactments have also affected patron rights, for example, libraries must now make reasonable accommodations for patrons with disabilities (Chapter 7). Many states now have statutes protecting the confidentiality of library patrons' circulation records (Chapter 6).

The change in the courts' role, however, is not simply the result of new interpretations of the state or federal constitutions or even because of new legislative enactments or administrative actions. The change is more significantly the result of the important role libraries have come to play in our modern democratic society and the decisions by library boards, librarians, and library organizations to accept this historic imperative by expanding the services offered by libraries and by making libraries as accessible as possible to everyone.

THE CHANGING ROLES OF LIBRARIES

Ancient Libraries

The earliest libraries were private collections of rare, one-of-a-kind items made of fragile materials such as clay tablets or papyrus rolls that required special care. The primary function of ancient libraries was to preserve and to protect these unique materials. Very often the loss of a particular item meant the work was lost forever. The private nature of these libraries was not the only reason that they had few patrons. Only members of a small, privileged class had the ability to read and the leisure time to use these collections.

The first library available to the public was in ancient Greece. The chief functions of this and other Greek libraries, however, was still largely to preserve and to protect their precious and unique collections. The ancient Greeks felt that stories passed orally from one generation to another, with each adding its own contributions, must be carefully recorded. The works of philosophers, historians, and scientists were also honored and added to by other members of their schools. Plays had to be preseved when they were no longer performed. Differences in interpretation and views in all fields must also be recorded. The tradition of public debate began with the Greek city-states, and written works aided in the creation of an educated and informed citizenry that was prepared for such lively debates.

When these few libraries were destroyed by war or natural disasters their works were completely lost unless small fragments could be found elsewhere. Several ancient works exist today only as references or quotations in the works of others.

Roman libraries, however, expanded upon the role of preserving their own culture. They created their collections with works taken from conquered nations, and Roman philosophers, scientists and statesmen used these works and built upon them. Roman citizens by necessity also had a strong interest in other cultures and in entertainment. Libraries came to be used more for both research and recreation—creating an even greater interest in new and novel works.

It was also in Rome that, for the first time in history, artists and authors were actually able to sell their own works. However, this recognition that the creator of a work owned it had only a brief moment in the ancient and medieval worlds. As we will see later, it was not really until passage of the first copyright law in 1710 that this right was again recognized.

Medieval Libraries

In the Middle Ages monks carefully preserved manuscripts by laboriously copying and illuminating them. In this period books were still very rare and very valuable. They were also seen by few people. As in the ancient world, ownership of books remained with the possessor of the work, who controlled what could be copied and what could not be. In fact, in the medieval scriptorium, a complex set of rules existed to determine:

- what works could or could not be copied;
- by whom they could be copied; and
- for whom they could be copied.

It was in this period that the first copyright case was heard by the courts. A copy of a manuscript had been made without its owner's consent. The court ruled that the copy must be returned to the original manuscript's owner, making its decision on the basis of property law. In the court's words: "to every cow her calf."

Renaissance

As Europe emerged from the Middle Ages and made the transition to the modern age, the classical works of the past helped revive the interest in new thoughts and ideas. This flourishing of the arts and sciences can be directly traced to rediscovery of the works that had been so carefully preserved and protected. Without access to these earlier works it is hard to see how this rebirth could have happened.[4]

The Printing Press

Before the invention of the printing press and the ability to produce large numbers of copies, the primary function of the few libraries that existed was still to preserve and protect their small, rare collections. Access to libraries was limited in order to protect the collections. The ownership of books also largely remained with the one who physically possessed the title. Creators had few if any rights to reproduce or distribute their own writings. There were thus few reasons to make copies of a work widely available. The owner of a rare and valuable title had little incentive to make it less valuable by freely letting others copy it. Authors who wished to have their works widely available simply did not have the means of doing so.

Following the invention of the printing press, libraries began to increase in size and number as books became less expensive and more available. National libraries were established in many countries, and the interest in books and literary works increased. Libraries also found new roles. They began to promote the growth of:

- literacy;
- access to information; and
- availability of books and reading material.

Even with the increasing availability of books, however, the rights to copy and publish did not immediately rest with their authors. In England, authors were not allowed to print and market their own works. In fact, only members of a specific guild of printers and booksellers, the Company of Stationers, were given the right by the Crown to print and sell books.[5] All others were barred, and those who failed to have their presses certified risked their destruction and a year's imprisonment. The penalty for even selling non-approved works was three months' imprisonment. The reason behind this was fear of the new technology: the Crown was concerned that a free press would result in the spread of sedition and revolution.[6]

First Copyright Law

Passage of the first copyright law was an important event for libraries and for the public's access to information. Except for that brief moment in Rome already cited, authors did not previously have the right to sell or distribute their own works. Behind the passage of this act was the belief that the best way to encourage creative activity was to give authors the rights to the fruits of their labor. The most immediate reason for the passage of the law, however, was the common sight in England of popular authors living in poverty and their families ending up in the poorhouses.

The first copyright law was known as the Statute of Queen Anne. Its full title is "A Bill for the Encouragement of Learning, by Vesting the Copies of Printed Books in the Authors or Purchasers of Such Copies, during the Times therein mentioned," and it took effect on April 10, 1710. The act began with the following statement of purpose:

> Whereas Printers, Booksellers, and other Persons have of late frequently taken the Liberty of printing, reprinting, and publishing or causing to be printed, reprinted, and published books, and other Writings, without Consent of the Authors or Proprietors of such Books and writings, to their great Detriment, and too often to the Ruin of them and their Families: preventing therefore such Practices for the future, and for the Encouragement of learned men to compose and write useful Books, may it please Your Majesty, that it may be enacted. . . .

This statute remains the foundation of copyright law in England and the United States today.[7]

One of the immediate benefits to libraries of early copyright laws was the requirement that copies of works must be deposited in a national or university library. The reason for this deposit requirement was to ensure that an untainted copy of a work could be found in the event an infringement suit was later brought in the courts. The deposit requirement was the principal means by which many great library collections were built and even today remains one of the chief means by which the Library of Congress acquires materials.

American Revolution

In the early American colonies libraries were largely private and books were relatively scarce. As it had been throughout previous history, access to information was largely limited to those who could afford it. The American Revolution and the Constitution changed this. Information, particularly information about the workings of government, would no longer be accessible only to the few. This was principally because the fundamental role of government had been changed and with it the historic mission of libraries.

LIBRARIES AND THE CONSTITUTION

Before coming to America the colonists had seen at first hand the abuses of sovereign governments in Europe, and in fact many had crossed the ocean to escape the religious and political persecutions of such governments. Prior to the American Revolution, the British government had also resorted to repressive means to prevent the loss of its American colonies. Severe restrictions were placed on freedom of religion, press, assembly, and speech in an unsuccessful attempt to suppress the insurrection. These experiences convinced the colonists that there had to be a new, different kind of government.

It is this revolutionary change in the role of government that is primarily responsible for U.S. citizens' unprecedented access to information. Under the British, the Crown was sovereign and the people were subjects. Under the Constitution, it is the people, not the government, that possess absolute sovereignty. The people held the power to censor over government, not the government over the people. Government could no longer limit access to information without a compelling and significant reason.

In addition, this revolution required an educated populace, citizens who were informed and capable of governing themselves. There must be vigorous debate in order to find the best solutions to the problems facing the young country. As the colonists had learned, truth is more likely to be gathered out of a multitude of tongues than through any kind of authoritative pronouncement. As Justice Holmes stated in a 1919 U.S. Supreme Court decision: the "best test of truth is the power of the thought to get itself accepted in the competition of the market. . . . "[8] It is for this reason that debate on public issues should be uninhibited, robust, and wide open, and may well include vehement, caustic, and sometimes unpleasant attacks.[9]

There are obvious risks to government in encouraging such "unfettered interchange of ideas,"[10] but the experiences of the colonists convinced them that it was far more hazardous to discourage thought. Only such open public debate could bring about desirable political and social changes in a lawful manner.[11] The safest path was not through repression but through the opportunity to discuss freely grievances and remedies.[12]

Under such a government the state must make it possible for its citizens to fully develop their reading and reasoning skills. Citizens must have access to new, different, and challenging thoughts and ideas. As the Court stated, "[T]he greatest menace to freedom is an inert people. . . ."[13] In a 1927 concurring opinion Justices Brandeis and Holmes gave this view a classic formulation that deserves to be quoted in full:

> Those who won our independence believed that the final end of the State was to make men free to develop their faculties; and that in its government the deliberative forces should prevail over the arbitrary. They believed that freedom to think as you will and to speak as you think are means indispensable to the discovery and spread of political truth; that without free speech and assembly discussion would be futile; that with them, discussion affords ordinarily adequate protection against the dissemination of noxious doctrine; that the greatest menace to freedom is an inert people. . . .[14]

Democratic governments are established to encourage self-actualization (the freedom to develop one's faculties), liberty (both as an end and a means), truth (freedom to think and to speak are indispensable to finding the truth), and freedom to change (inertia is the greatest enemy). Throughout American history, the public library was and still remains the principal means of achieving these ends.

These ideals were exemplified in the life of James Madison, the chief architect of the Constitution. Madison voiced the need for public libraries throughout his long public career because he believed that an informed citizenry is the best means of preserving democratic liberties. His words are inscribed on walls of the Madison Memorial Hall in the Library of Congress:

Learned institutions ought to be favorite objects with every free people. They throw that light over the public mind which is the best security against crafty and dangerous encroachments on the public liberty.[15]

How the Courts View the Role of Libraries

Both state and federal courts have affirmed that establishing and maintaining a public library is among the highest functions of government. The principal reason given by the courts has been the role libraries perform in educating and informing the public in a democratic society.

In January 1930 the Court of Appeals of Maryland, the state's highest court, considered an appeal from the condemnation of a parcel of land to erect a free public library building in Baltimore. After determining that all of the procedural requirements had been met, the court turned to the issue of whether a free public library serves an important enough municipal purpose to justify the taking of this private property. To this question the court responded that there can be no more important duty or purpose for a state or municipality than to provide a free public library for its residents. The court reasoned that it is widely acknowledged that libraries are an integral part of a public education and such education must not stop when formal schooling ends. Citizens must continually read and study to keep abreast, particularly under a democratic form of government. "An enlightened and educated public has come to be regarded as the surest safeguard" for the advancement of civilized nations, and libraries are the most "efficient and valuable" means of ensuring such enlightenment.[16]

In April 1945 the U.S. Circuit Court of Appeals affirmed the reasoning and conclusions of the Court of Appeals of Maryland from fifteen years earlier but in a case with an entirely different set of circumstances. The federal court's case involved an applicant who complained that she had been denied admission to a training class at a public library because of her race. Exclusion from this training course, which often led to employment in the library, would deprive the applicant of the equal protection of the law in violation of the Constitution and the Civil Rights Act. The discrimination was not in doubt. The question facing the court was whether the library had government status and thus was subject to suit in the federal courts. The court acknowledged and quoted with approval the Maryland Court of Appeals' reasoning: "It is generally recognized that the maintenance of a public library is a proper function of the state. . . ."[17]

In March 1945 the Court of Appeals of Kentucky considered

the issue of whether the state legislature had the power to compel a municipality to levy a tax to support a public library. The court concluded that the legislature did indeed have such power under the state's constitution. The principal reasons are that a public library is a government function and that the benefits of a local library extend beyond the local community in which it is located. In reaching this conclusion, the court rejected the arguments of the city's lawyers that public libraries are only a place of amusement where the public finds relaxation and enjoyment to pass away the time in a "realm separate and apart from the realities and drab sameness of everyday existence." While the court admitted that some library patrons do find the library a place to relax and be relieved of the "cares that infest the day," this is not idle amusement. On the contrary, the court said, it is amusement that best prepares individuals to be of service to their neighbors, city, state, and nation. The library patron spreads knowledge, helps lift the "ban of ignorance, and stimulates a desire on the part of his associates to improve their own minds, thus advancing the cultural status of the community."[18]

In the court's opinion, libraries also provide a place for extracurricular research to supplement the classroom. Libraries make it possible for those who no longer attend school to complete their education. Libraries raise the standard of knowledge and education.

> It may be likened to a mirror wherein, delving, one may see a reflection of the past. Were we not permitted to gaze into the past, our civilization long since would have marked its own time by being required to investigate anew each approach to a particular field of investigation or line of thought, and actually to blunder by the repetition of mistakes so clearly demonstrated in the written records.[19]

Such an institution is educational in every aspect and thus a proper function of government.

Courts in other states have also recognized the valuable, civic nature of libraries. In 1938 the Texas Court of Civil Appeals considered whether a library could be erected on a piece of land that was deeded to the city of Fort Worth for a park. In making its determination, the court held that a library is not a playground for children. In fact such activities would be a nuisance to someone who uses a public library for its intended purposes. A library is a repository for knowledge, a place for study and research, and a place that affords "sane recreation." It is not a park.[20]

Even the U.S. Supreme Court has recognized the importance

of libraries. In 1966 the Court reviewed convictions by the Louisiana courts in a civil rights context of five black men for violating a breach of the peace statute. The case involved a peaceful protest in a racially segregated public library. Justice Fortas in the majority opinion immediately noted that because the protest occurred in a public library and might involve questions that are materially different from other protests, the Court heard arguments and considered the case *in extenso*.[21]

The Court noted that the protesters' presence in the library was unquestionably lawful. "It was a public facility, open to the public."[22] The protesters were polite and remained in the library for only ten or fifteen minutes. The library room was empty except for the librarians. There were no onlookers and the protesters did nothing even remotely provocative. The Court saw that the protest involved First Amendment constitutional rights but was upset that the incident occurred in a library. "It is an unhappy circumstance that the locus of these events was a public library—a place dedicated to quiet, to knowledge, and to beauty. It is a sad commentary that this hallowed place . . . bore the ugly stamp of racism."[23] More significantly, the Court noted that there was "no disturbance of others, no disruption of library activities, and no violation of any library regulation."[24] If such a disruption had occurred, the Court would have had to consider this in the charge of breach of the peace.

In sum, although the courts have not actually defined what a public library is, they have at all levels—state and federal, trial and appellate—acknowledged the important historic and constitutional role that libraries play in a democratic society. Throughout history, libraries have played a key role in preserving and making information available. Libraries have also promoted reading and the availability of books and other educational media. The courts have acknowledged the additional role for libraries of providing access to the knowledge and skills necessary for a people to wisely govern themselves.

First Amendment

The provision of the Constitution that most clearly defines this new role for libraries is the First Amendment. The purposes behind the First Amendment are best met by the public library. Only libraries can provide the uncompromised and unequivocal access to the broad range and kinds of information needed by an enlightened electorate. It is, however, an irony that it is also the First

Amendment rights of patrons that can conflict with library rules and regulations that are essential to the effective operation of a library.

ENDNOTES

1. For a history of the development of the constitutional right to receive information and ideas see Chapter 2 of the authors' *Maintaining the Privacy of Library Records: A Handbook and Guide* (New York: Neal-Schuman, 1994).
2. Ibid., 34. See also Appendix C: "U.S. Supreme Court on the Constitutional Right to Privacy," pp. 185–88.
3. In *Brown* v. *Louisiana*, 383 U.S. 131 at 143 (1966), the Court stated:
   A State or its instrumentality may, of course, regulate the use of its libraries or other public facilities. But it must do so in a reasonable and nondiscriminatory manner, equally applicable to all and administered with equality to all. It may not do so as to some and not as to all. It may not provide certain facilities for whites and others for Negroes. And it may not invoke regulations as to use—whether they are *ad hoc* or general—as a pretext for pursuing those engaged in lawful, constitutionally protected exercise of their fundamental rights.
4. A excellent example of this is Euclid's Fifth Postulate. When Euclid formulated it around 1500 B.C., it aroused considerable controversy. Non-Euclidean geometry developed in 1826 as a result of the rediscovery of accounts of this original controversy.
5. Queen Mary Tudor chartered the Company of Stationers (Letter Patent of May 4, 1557) .
6. Hallam, 1 *Constitutional History* 238.
7. For a more detailed account of the history of copyright law see the previous volume in this series *Libraries and Copyright Law*.
8. Justice Holmes dissenting opinion in *Abrams* v. *United States*, 250 U.S. 616 at 630 (1919).
9. *Terminiello* v. *Chicago*, 337 U.S. 1 at 4 (1949).
10. *Roth* v. *United States*, 354 U.S. 476 at 484 (1957).
11. *Stromberg* v. *California*, 283 U.S. 359 at 369 (1931).
12. Justice Brandeis in a concurring opinion to *Whitney* v. *California*, 274 U.S. 357 at 375–76 (1927).
13. *Whitney* at 375 (1927).
14. Ibid.
15. From a letter dated Aug. 4, 1822 to W. T. Barry, Lieutenant Governor of Kentucky.
16. *Johnson* v. *Baltimore*, 158 Md. 93 at 103–104 (1930). The court actually said:
   At the present time it is generally recognized and conceded by all thoughtful people that such institutions form an integral part of

a system of free public education and are among its most efficient and valuable adjuncts. An enlightened and educated public has come to be regarded as the surest safeguard for the maintenance and advancement of the progress of civilized nations. More particularly is this true in republican forms of government, wherein all citizens have a voice. It is also true that education of the people ought not and does not stop upon their leaving school, but must be kept abreast of the time by almost constant reading and study. It would therefore seem that no more important duty or higher purpose is incumbent upon a state or municipality than to provide free public libraries for the benefits of its inhabitants.

17. *Kerr v. Enoch Pratt Free Library of Baltimore City*, 149 F.2d 212 at 217 (1945).

18. *Board of Trustees, Newport Public Library v. City of Newport*, 300 Ky.125 at 127 (1945). The court's exact words are:

Counsel for appellee takes the position that a public library is solely a place of amusement where its patrons indulge in moments of relaxation and enjoyment—"a kind of enjoyment to pass away the time in a realm separate and apart from the realities and drab sameness of everyday existence." It may be that some of the patrons experience this character of enjoyment upon their visitation to public libraries; and for them such institutions, indeed, are places wherein they may relax and be relieved of the "cares that infest the day." But such cannot be said to be idle amusement; on the contrary, it is one that better fits the individual to be of help to his neighbor, city, state, and nation. His contact with his fellowmen spreads knowledge, helps lift the ban of ignorance, and stimulates a desire on the part of his associates to improve their own minds, thus advancing the cultural status of the community. But irrespective of the beneficial effect to the public of this character of its use, we are not willing to concede that such is the sole function of a public library—it provides for the youth a medium for extra curricular research to supplement the basic principles taught in the classroom; it provides a facility for those to continue their education who, perforce, have abandoned attendance upon the public schools; and it is an institution which permits the adult, even though he may have completed the highest prescribed course of education, to continue his studies and improve his culture. In either event, the library raises the standard of knowledge and education. It may be likened to a mirror wherein, delving, one may see a reflection of the past. Were we not permitted to gaze into the future through this mirror of the past, our civilization long since would have marked its own time by being required to investigate anew each approach to a particular field of investigation or line of thought, and actually to blunder by the repetition of mistakes so clearly demonstrated in the written records. Each individual research serves as an enlightenment to the public at large. The institution which affords this opportunity is educational in its every aspect.

19. Ibid.
20. *City of Fort Worth* v. *Burnett*, 115 S.W. 2d 436 at 439–440 (1938).
21. *Brown* v. *Louisiana*, 383 U.S. 131 at 139 (1966).
22. Ibid. at 139.
23. Ibid. at 142.
24. Ibid.

2

The First Amendment

- *Are First Amendment rights absolute and inviolable?*
- *What were the motivating forces behind the adoption of the First Amendment so soon after the Constitution was ratified?*
- *Why has it taken so long for the courts to rule on the First Amendment rights of library patrons?*
- *Are there any rights in the First Amendment which are not immediately apparent?*

The rights and freedoms guaranteed by the First Amendment are central to our concept of liberty.[1] It is not, however, immediately apparent how the First Amendment can conflict with library use regulations. After all, libraries are essential to encouraging the informed debate that makes democracy possible, and librarians and library organizations have been at the forefront in defending First Amendment rights.

To understand the relationship between library patrons and the First Amendment, we must first look carefully at the First Amendment's history, language, and purposes. We must then determine how the U.S. Supreme Court has developed several doctrines not immediately apparent in the actual wording of the First Amendment.

HISTORY OF THE FIRST AMENDMENT

The First Amendment was not part of the U.S. Constitution as it was originally drafted in Philadelphia by the Constitutional Convention during the summer of 1787. However, after the U.S. Constitution was finally signed by the delegates on September 17, 1787, and submitted to the states for ratification, the lack of a bill of rights drew more public criticism than any other aspect of the Constitution. It soon became clear that the Constitution would not be ratified by the states without a firm assurance from its drafters that a bill of rights would be approved in the form of amendments to the new Constitution at the very first session of Congress.[2]

After the promise was made, the required nine states ratified the Constitution on June 21, 1788, with the explicit understanding that the new Congress would draft and recommend to the states the adoption of such a bill of rights. At that first session of Congress, the House of Representatives adopted seventeen proposed amendments to the Constitution. The Senate[3] reduced that number to twelve, which was then agreed to by the House and sent on to the states for ratification on September 25, 1789. Ten of the twelve amendments were ratified by 11 of 14 states and were added to the Constitution on December 15, 1791. The two unratified amendments dealt with the number of representatives in Congress and with the compensation of senators and representatives.[4] The First Amendment actually became first because these two prior amendments were not ratified.

LANGUAGE OF THE FIRST AMENDMENT

The United States Constitution, Amendment I, states that:

Congress shall make no law respecting an establishment of religion, or prohibiting the free exercise thereof; or abridging the freedom of speech, or of the press; or the right of the people peaceably to assemble, and to petition the Government for a redress of grievances.

Applicability

The first word, "Congress," would seem to limit the prohibitions of the First Amendment to the federal government, and for its first 137 years it did. However, the Fourteenth Amendment[5] to the Constitution, which was ratified in 1868, was determined by the U.S. Supreme Court in 1925[6] to make the rights in the First Amendment applicable to the states and all of their political subdivisions—counties, cities, towns, villages, and boroughs. This is one of the reasons that it has taken the courts so long to consider the First Amendment's relationship to libraries.

Unequivocal

The phrase "shall make no law" would appear to be mandatory, absolute, and without exceptions or limitations. "No" should, after all, mean "no." It is also the only provision of the Bill of Rights that contains no exceptions. The Fourth Amendment, for example, prohibits unreasonable searches except for those made on probable cause.[7]

In actuality, however, Congress has never accepted the First Amendment prohibitions as either absolute or inviolate. In 1798, just seven years after the First Amendment became part of the Constitution, Congress enacted the Sedition Act. Many scholars, government officials, and judges, including Thomas Jefferson, believed the statute clearly violated the First Amendment.[8] In 1940 Congress enacted the Alien Registration Act (Smith Act) and in 1950 the Subversive Control Act (McCarran Act). These acts violated the absolute prohibition against the enactment of laws limiting freedom of speech.

The U.S. Supreme Court has also never regarded First Amendment freedoms as absolute. Why would the Court and the Congress so steadfastly stand against what is clearly the plain and simple meaning of the First Amendment? There are several reasons:

- Exceptions to the Bill of Rights have always been recognized, even by the drafters of the Constitution and its amendments.[9]
- An absolute, unequivocal right without limitations or exceptions would not work. The Bill of Rights appears at the end of a constitution that sets up a federal government and is clearly not intended to replace it or to render it unworkable. Without a society maintaining public order, liberty would be lost in the excesses of anarchy.[10]
- An extreme, uncompromising position would lead to irreconcilable conflict between several of the clauses in the First Amendment itself.

Only two Justices, Hugo L. Black and William O. Douglas, have held that the First Amendment absolutely means what it says. Both their views were expressed in dissenting opinions. Justice Black, a consistent advocate of the absolutist position, in a 1952 case stated, "I do not agree that the Constitution leaves freedom of petition, assembly, speech, press or worship at the mercy of a case-by-case, day-by-day majority of this Court . . . . I think the First Amendment with the Fourteenth, 'absolutely' forbids such laws without 'ifs' or 'buts' or 'whereases'."[11]

In a 1973 case, Justice Douglas noted in his dissenting opinion, "The First Amendment is written in terms that are absolute. Its command is that 'Congress shall make no law . . . abridging the freedom of speech or of the press. . . .' The ban of 'no' law that abridges freedom of the press is in my view total and complete."[12] Justice Douglas did not, however, hold this view in all instances. In 1950, he stated in a dissenting opinion: "The freedom to speak is not absolute."[13] In 1966, in another dissenting opinion, he recognized that there is a time, place and manner limitation on freedom of speech. "No one, for example, would suggest that the Senate gallery is the proper place for a vociferous protest rally."[14]

Rights and Liberties

The remainder of the text of the First Amendment can be separated into three fundamental and interconnected rights. These are the rights to be free from government interference in:

- religion;
- expression (speech and press); and
- assembly and petition.

These rights comprise fundamental liberties that are essential to the pursuit of happiness. They are the very rights and freedoms that the Declaration of Independence declared to be inalienable and for which governments are instituted.[15]

RELIGION

"Congress shall make no law respecting an establishment of religion, or prohibiting the free exercise thereof. . . ."[16] This creates two distinct prohibitions: one relating to the "establishment" of religion and the second to the "free exercise" of religion. The first prohibition, which has come to be known as the Establishment Clause, has the practical effect of excluding the federal government and the states from acting in the area of religion. Federal and state governments must remain neutral in matters of religion. They may not set up a church or pass laws that aid one religion, aid all religions, or prefer one religion over another.[17] In Jefferson's words, the clause was intended to erect "a wall of separation between church and state."[18] The second prohibition, known as the Free Exercise Clause, bars government regulation of religious beliefs as such.[19] It prohibits government from discrimination against an individual or group because of religious views or beliefs and from compelling persons to affirm any particular religious belief in conflict with their own.[20]

Both the Establishment and Free Exercise Clauses resulted from early Americans' experiences with government-supported religions. Many of the early settlers came from Europe to escape laws that compelled them to support and attend government favored churches. They saw firsthand the turmoil, civil strife, and persecutions that came about in part because a country's predominant religious sect was determined to maintain its absolute political and religious supremacy. "In efforts to force loyalty to whatever religious group happened to be on top and in league with the government of a particular time and place, men and women had been fined, cast in jail, cruelly tortured, and killed."[21]

Offenses that were so severely punished included merely speaking disrespectfully of the views of ministers of government-established churches, nonattendance at those churches, expressions of nonbelief, and the failure to pay taxes to support those churches. These practices continued even in the New World. Colonists who belonged to a minority sect were persecuted because they worshipped as their conscience dictated. These experiences created the conviction that individual religious liberty could be achieved best under a government stripped of all power to tax, support, or assist any or all religions, or to interfere with the beliefs of any religious individual or group.[22]

The union of government and religion also tends to destroy government and to degrade religion. The history of governmentally-established religion, both in England and in America, showed that whenever government had allied itself with one particular religion, the inevitable result had been the hatred, disrespect, and even contempt of those who held contrary beliefs. History has also shown that many people lost their respect for any religion that relied upon the support of government to spread its faith.[23]

As it has with the other freedoms guaranteed under the First Amendment, the Court has not interpreted or applied the Religion Clauses in the absolute terms in which they are written. One cannot, for example, refuse to testify in court because of religious beliefs, even if it violates the tenets of his or her faith.[24] A religious congregation cannot violate a local zoning ordinance that prohibits construction of church buildings in residential districts even if it means the congregation cannot construct a building on a lot it owns.[25]

The Court has also struggled to find a neutral course between the two clauses themselves because they, if carried to their logical extreme, would clash with each other. For example, paying an army chaplain with federal funds might be said to violate the Establishment Clause. However, soldiers stationed at a faraway outpost could complain that a government that did not provide a chaplain was prohibiting them from the free exercise of their religion.[26] Rigidity would thus thwart the basic function of these clauses.[27]

It is clear that Americans will not tolerate either a government-established religion or government interference with religion.[28] Short of these prohibitions, however, the Court has sought to find room for neutrality. "The First Amendment . . . does not say that in every and all respects there shall be a separation of Church and State."[29] Indeed, as a practical matter there can be no such complete and uncompromising separation:

- In 1947 the Court upheld a state statute that reimbursed the parents of parochial school children for bus transportation expenses.[30]
- In 1968 the Court upheld the state loans of textbooks to parochial schools.[31]
- In 1952 the Court approved the release during school hours of pupils to go to religious centers for religious instructions.[32]

However, four years earlier, the Court had voided a program establishing a period during which pupils in public schools were to be allowed to receive religious instruction.[33] The difference turned on the programs being conducted off school property. In this case, as in others when the Court is confronted with a conflict between secular interests and religious rights, the Justices asked not only if the government's purpose is sufficiently compelling but also if the means government chooses to achieve that goal have been narrowly tailored to respect those religious rights.[34] The Court will also test to see if the law has a secular legislative purpose, if the law's primary effect advances or inhibits religion, and if the law fosters an excessive government entanglement with religion.[35]

In regard to the Free Exercise Clause, the Court has also attempted to draw a distinction between belief and conduct. The freedom to believe is absolute, but the freedom to act may be limited. A state or local government can by general and nondiscriminatory legislation regulate time, place, and manner and may in other ways safeguard the peace, order, and comfort of the community without unconstitutionally invading the beliefs of its citizens.[36] The Free Exercise Clause thus does not include the right to violate statutory laws or maintain a nuisance. "The fact that one acts from the promptings of religious beliefs does not immunize against lawless conduct."[37]

Expression

The clause that now reads "Congress shall make no laws . . . abridging the freedom of speech, or of the press" was introduced into the House of Representatives on June 8, 1789 as: "The people shall not be deprived or abridged of their right to speak, to write, or to publish their sentiments; and the freedom of the press, as one of the great bulwarks of liberty, shall be inviolable."[38] It was amended and given its final form in the Senate. It is unclear from the records of the Constitutional Convention or from the debate in the House what the framers' real purposes were behind the freedoms of speech and the press. There is no record of any debate in the Senate or in the states during ratification. The lack of interest in debate is probably because the amendment was not seen as a novel governmental principle but rather the continuation of rights guaranteed from the country's English ancestry.[39] Because of this the Court has been required to identify the purposes behind the Speech and Press Clauses. One of the most important and unquestioned[40] of these purposes is to ensure "unfettered interchange of ideas for the bringing about of political and social changes desired by the people."[41]

The Court has not interpreted or applied the Speech and Press Clauses in the absolute terms in which they are written. Freedom of speech and freedom of the press do not confer an absolute right to speak or publish without responsibility. For one, it does not mean that anyone with an opinion or belief may address a group at any public place and at any time.[42] No one can ignore a red light as a means of social protest, and no one would defend a street meeting in the middle of Times Square at rush hour as a form of freedom of speech.

Limitations and exceptions were recognized by the drafters of the clauses themselves. Libel and obscenity were never seen as falling within the constitutionally protected area of speech. Obscenity was excluded because it had nothing to do with unfettered interchange of ideas for the bringing about of political or social changes.[43] Obscenity did not play an essential part in the exposition of ideas and was of such slight social value that any benefit from it was outweighed by the social interest in order and morality.[44]

Despite these limitations, the practical effect of the Speech and Press Clauses is to bar most prior restraint of expression. It also limits subsequent punishment to a very narrow range of expression.

Press

In early America, freedom of the press meant immunity from prior restraint or censorship.[45] Under the English system all printers were licensed, and nothing could be published without the prior approval of the state or church. The great struggle for freedom of the press was thus for the right to publish without a license that which for a long time could be published only with a license.[46]

The purpose of the Press Clause was stated in a 1774 letter of the Continental Congress to the inhabitants of Quebec:

> The last right we shall mention regards the freedom of the press. The importance of this consists, besides the advancement of truth, science, morality, and arts in general, in its diffusion of liberal sentiments on the administration of Government, its ready communication of thoughts between subjects, and its consequential promotion of union among them, whereby oppressive officers are shamed or intimidated, into more honorable and just modes of conducting affairs.[47]

The Court thus acknowledged the role of the press in scrutinizing closely the conduct of public affairs and has made it clear that just because freedom of the press can be abused does not make it any less necessary. Subsequent punishment for abuses, not prior restraint, is the appropriate remedy.[48] Only in exceptional circumstances is prior restraint permitted. The only discretion that public officials should have in issuing permits should be related to questions of time, place, and manner.[49]

Assembly and Petition

"Congress shall make no law . . . abridging . . . the right of the people peaceably to assemble, and to petition the Government for a redress of grievances." These rights are closely related in origin and purpose with the rights of free speech and free press. Like the Speech and Press Clauses, the purpose of this clause is to ensure freedom of communication on matters related to the functioning of government.[50] The very idea of government in the United States implies a right of citizens to meet peaceably to discuss and consult on public affairs and to petition the government for a redress of grievances.[51] It is was thus not by accident or coincidence that the clauses were coupled. Freedom of speech and the press and the right to assemble and petition are inseparable rights, or, in the words of the Court, they are "cognate rights."[52]

The right of petition existed long before the Constitution. Deeply rooted in English traditions, the right can be traced to Magna Carta of 1215, and it appeared in the English Bill of Rights of 1689.[53] The right of petition also appeared prior to the Constitutional Convention in the Declarations of Rights of several state constitutions, including that of Pennsylvania.[54] Under English law, however, the right to assemble was considered as merely instrumental to the right of petition. The First Amendment makes these two rights equally fundamental. Under the First Amendment and in the view of the Court neither right can be denied without violating the fundamental principles of liberty and justice that are the base of all civil and political institutions.[55]

The rights are also not limited to religious and political grievances. The right to assemble, for example, protects the right to discuss and inform people concerning the advantages and disadvantages of unions.[56] The right of petition for redress of grievances is not limited to government officials and legislatures, but also includes the courts.[57] This right is not limited to a redress for grievances; it includes the right to demand that government use its powers to further the interests of the petitioners and of their views on politically contentious matters.[58]

Like other First Amendment rights, however, the rights to assemble and to petition are not absolute. They are limited in the same way as freedom of speech and press. For example, they offer no immunity from damages for libel.[59] The Court has made it clear, however, that any attempt to limit these liberties must be justified by a clear public interest. If the discussion is orderly and at an appropriate time and place, only a real or impending danger can be used to justify its limitation. In the Court's view there must be the widest room for discussion and the narrowest range for its restriction.[60] Mere public intolerance or animosity is not enough. "The First and Fourteenth Amendment do not permit a State to make criminal the exercise of the right of assembly simply because its exercise may be 'annoying' to some people."[61] After all, debate on public issues should be uninhibited, robust, and wide open.[62]

PENUMBRAL RIGHTS

In addition to the rights specifically enumerated in the language of the First Amendment, the Court has recognized several additional rights as being essential. These peripherial rights are described by the Court in a term used to discuss eclipses and sunspots. The dark area of a eclipse or sunspot is called the *umbra*.

Between this absolute dark area and the full light is an area of partial shadow known as the *penumbra*. In a 1965 case[63] the Court stated that the specific guarantees in the First Amendment and in the rest of the Bill of Rights have "penumbras." These penumbral rights are formed by emanations from the specific guarantees, and it is those specific guarantees that give penumbral rights their life and substance.

The right of citizens to use a public library and to have their library records kept confidential is not guaranteed by any explicitedly enumerated right in the First Amendment. There are, however, three penumbral rights that emanate from the First Amendment that do relate to these patrons' rights. The first of these is the constitutional right to receive information and ideas. This right is treated in Chapter 3. The second is the constitutional right of association, and the third is constitutional right to privacy. These two doctrines are dealt with in Chapter 5.

ENDNOTES

1. As the U.S. Supreme Court stated in 1920: "That freedom of speech and of the press are elements of liberty all will acclaim. Indeed they are so intimate to liberty in every one's convictions—we may say feelings—that there is an instinctive and instant revolt from any limitation of them by law . . . ." *Schaefer* v. *United States*, 251 U.S. 466 at 474 (1920).

2. *West Virginia State Board of Education* v. *Barnette,* 319 U.S. 624 at 637 (1943) at 637.

3. One of the amendments rejected by the Senate read: "The equal rights of conscience, the freedom of speech or of the press, and the right of trial by jury in criminal cases shall not be infringed by any State." James Madison declared that this amendment was "the most valuable of the whole list." 1 *Annals of Congress* 755 (August 17, 1789). The restrictions of the First Amendment were not declared to apply to the states by the U.S. Supreme Court until 1925.

4. The amendment relating to compensation of representatives was finally adopted as the 27th Amendment to the Constitution on May 19, 1992, 203 years after it was submitted to the states.

5. The specific clause is "nor shall any State deprive any person of life, liberty, or property, without due process of law. . . ."

6. "For present purposes we may and do assume that freedom of speech and of the press—which are protected by the First Amendment from abridgment by Congress—are among the fundamental personal rights and 'liberties' protected by the due process clause of the Fourteenth Amendment from impairment by the States." *Gitlow* v. *New York*, 268

U.S. 652 at 666 (1925).

7. The Fourth Amendment states: "The right of the people to be secure in their persons, houses, papers, and effects, against unreasonable searches and seizures, shall not be violated, and no warrants shall issue, but upon probable cause, supported by oath or affirmation, and particularly describing the place to be searched, and the persons or things to be seized."

8. Supreme Court Justice Douglas in 1973 also thought the acts were unconstitutional. *Columbia Broadcasting* v. *Democratic Committee*, 412 U.S. 94 at 156 (1973).

9. *Robertson* at 281. Consider also Justice Frankfurter's concurring opinion in *Dennis* v. *United States* (1951):

    ... there are those who find in the Constitution a wholly unfettered right of expression. Such literalness treats the words of the Constitution as though they were found on a piece of outworn parchment instead of being words that have called into being a nation with a past to be preserved for the future. The soil in which the Bill of Rights grew was not a soil of arid pedantry. The historic antecedents of the First Amendment preclude the notion that its purpose was to give unqualified immunity to every expression that touched on matters within the range of political interest.

    341 U.S. 494 at 521 (1951).

10. *Cox* v. *Louisiana*, 379 U.S. 536 at 554 (1965).

11. *Beauharnais* v. *Illinois*, 343 U.S. 250 at 274–275 (1952). Dissenting opinion.

12. *Columbia Broadcasting* at 156 (1973).

13. *Dennis* at 581 (1950).

14. *Adderley* v. *Florida*, 385 U.S. 39 at 54 (1966).

15. The exact words are:

    We hold these truths to be self-evident, that all men are created equal, that they are endowed by their Creator with certain unalienable Rights, that among these are Life, Liberty, and the pursuit of Happiness. . .That to secure these rights, Governments are instituted among Men, deriving their just powers from the consent of the governed, That whenever any Form of Government becomes destructive of these ends, it is the Right of the People to alter or to abolish it, Band to institute new Government, laying its foundation on such principles and organizing its powers in such form, as to them shall seem most likely to effect their Safety and Happiness.

16. The original language of the First Amendment clause relating to religion was, "The civil rights of none shall be abridged on account of religious belief or worship, nor shall any national religion be established, nor shall the full and equal right of conscience be in any manner, or any pretense, infringed." 1 *Annals of Congress* 434 (June 8, 1789). In the Senate and House Conference, the current language was adopted.

17. *Everson* v. *Board of Education*, 330 U.S. 1 at 15 (1947).

18. Ibid.
19. In 1993 the Religious Freedom Restoration Act was enacted. This law was a direct reaction to the U.S. Supreme Court case *Employment Division* v. *Smith*, 494 U.S. 872 (1990). This case came to be known as the "Peyote Case." Congress wanted to "restore" the compelling interest test. Since its passage the statute has been challenged on the grounds that the Court has the duty to determine what the Constitution says.
20. *Braunfield* v. *Brown*, 366 U.S. 599 (1961).
21. *Everson* at 9.
22. Ibid. at 11.
23. *Engel* v. *Vitale*, 370 U.S. 421 at 431 (1962).
24. *State* v. *Bing*, 253 S.E.2d 101 at 102 (1979).
25. *Lakewood, Ohio Congregation of Jehovah's Witnesses, Inc.* v. *City of Lakewood*, Ohio, 699 F.2d 303 at 305 (1983).
26. This example is used by Justice Stewart in his dissenting opinion in *Sherbert* v. *Verner*, 374 U.S. 398.
27. *Walz* v. *Tax Commission*, 397 U.S. 664 at 669 (1970).
28. In *West Virginia State Board of Education* at 642, the Court said that "If there is any fixed star in our constitutional constellation, it is that no official, high or petty, can prescribe what shall be orthodox in politics, nationalism, religion, or other matters of opinion. . . ."
29. *Zorach* v. *Clauson*, 343 U.S. 306 at 312 (1952).
30. *Everson* at 1.
31. *Board of Education* v. *Allen*, 392 U.S. 236 at 243 (1968).
32. *Zorach* at 306.
33. *Illinois ex rel. McCollum* v. *Board of Education*, 333 U.S. 203 (1948).
34. *Africa* v. *Anderson*, 542 F.Supp. 224 at 228 (1982). In *Cantwell* at 304, the Court stated that: "In every case the power to regulate must be so exercised as not, in attaining a permissible end, unduly to infringe the protected freedom."
35. *Lemon* v. *Kurtzman*, 403 U.S. 602 at 612–3 (1971).
36. *Cantwell*, at 304.
37. *State ex rel. Swann* v. *Pack*, 527 S.W. 2d 99 at 111 (1975). Affirmed by the U.S. Supreme Court at 424 U.S. 954 (1975).
38. 1 *Annals of Congress* 434 (1789).
39. 165 U.S. 275 at 281 (1897).
40. In *Mills* v. *Alabama*, 384 U.S. 214 at 219 (1966) the Court stated that: "Whatever differences may exist about interpretations of the First Amendment, there is practically universal agreement that a major purpose of that Amendment was to protect the free discussion of governmental affairs."
41. *Roth* v. *United States*, 354 U.S. 476 at 484 (1957).
42. *Cox* v. *Louisiana*, 379 U.S. 536 at 554 (1965).
43. *Roth* at 484.
44. *Chaplinsky* v. *New Hampshire*, 315 U.S. 568 at 571–572 (1942).
45. *Near* v. *Minnesota ex rel. Olson*, 283 U.S. 697 at 716 (1931).
46. *Near*, at 713–714.

47. 1 *Journals of the Continental Congress* 108 (1774) quoted in *Roth* at 484.

48. As stated in *Near* at 719–720:

     [T]he administration of government has become more complex, the opportunities for malfeasance and corruption have multiplied, crime has grown to most serious proportions, and the danger of its protection by unfaithful officials and of the impairment of the fundamental security of life and property by criminal alliances and official neglect, emphasizes the primary need of a vigilant and courageous press, especially in great cities. The fact that the liberty of the press may be abused by miscreant purveyors of scandal does not make any the less necessary the immunity of the press from previous restraint in dealing with official misconduct. Subsequent punishment for such abuses as may exist is the appropriate remedy, consistent with constitutional privilege.

49. *Cox* v. *New Hampshire*, 312 U.S. 569 (1941).

50. *Richmond Newspapers, Inc.* v. *Virginia*, 448 U.S. 555 at 575 (1980).

51. *De Jonge* v. *State of Oregon*, 299 U.S. 353 at 552–553 (1937).

52. *Thomas* v. *Collins*, 323 U.S. 516 at 530 (1945).

53. "[I]t is the Right of the Subjects to petition the King." 1 Wm. & Mary, Sess 2, ch 2.

54. *McDonald* v. *Smith*, 472 U.S. 479 at 483–484 (1985).

55. *De Jonge* at 364–365.

56. *Thomas* at 531.

57. *Rhem* v. *McGrath*, 326 F.Supp 681 at 680 (1971).

58. *Eastern R.R. Presidents Conference* v. *Noerr Motor Freight*, 365 U.S. 127 (1961).

59. *McDonald* v. *Smith*, 472 U.S. 479 at 483 (1985).

60. *Thomas* at 530.

61. *Coates* v. *Cincinnati*, 402 U.S. 611 at 615 (1971).

62. *New York Times Co.* v. *Sullivan*, 376 U.S. 254 at 270 (1964) at 270.

63. *Griswold* v. *Connecticut*, 381 U.S. 479 (1965).

3

Right to Receive Information and Ideas

- *Where can the constitutional right to receive information and ideas be found?*
- *Why is this right particularly important to the rights of library patrons?*
- *Does this right protect the confidentiality of library records?*

The right to receive information and ideas derives from the First Amendment. While not actually mentioned in the words of the amendment, this right is so essential to its fullest exercise that it must be considered a necessary penumbral right.

For libraries, the constitutional right to receive information and ideas is one of the most important of the First Amendment's penumbral rights. This right confirms that the First Amendment does more than prohibit government from enacting laws that censor information; it also encompasses a positive right of public access to information and ideas. In 1992, the Third Circuit U.S. Court of Appeals decided one of the most important cases dealing with the rights of library patrons. This case was not appealed and is therefore law in the Third Circuit (which includes the states of New Jersey, Pennsylvania, and Delware). The circuit court stated that the constitutional right to receive information and ideas "includes the right to some level of access to a public library, the quintessential locus of the receipt of information."[1] As we will also see, a library censorship case also figures prominently in the development of the right itself.

In this chapter we will consider whether the constitutional right to receive information and ideas protects patrons' right of access to a public library, the confidentiality of library records, and against censorship of library collections. To determine this we will first have to look carefully at the development of this right. Like other First Amendment rights, the right to receive information and ideas can be traced historically through the opinions of the U.S. Supreme Court.

HISTORICAL DEVELOPMENT

1943

In *Martin* v. *City of Struthers*[2] the Court decided for the first time that freedom to speak also included the right to receive speech. This case considered the constitutionality of a municipal ordinance of the city of Struthers, Ohio, that forbade any person from knocking on the door, ringing the doorbell, or otherwise summoning the occupants of any residence for the purpose of distributing handbills or circulars to them. The purpose of the ordinance was to protect residents from annoyance and to prevent crime. The city of Struthers was at that time an industrial community where most of its residents worked in the iron and steel industry. Many worked on night shifts and slept during the day. In addition, it was noted that burglars often pose as canvassers in order to discover if a house is empty or to determine which one to rob.

Ms. Martin, a Jehovah's Witness, admitted distributing leaflets about a meeting of her religious group by knocking on doors in the city in violation of the ordinance. Even though she had proceeded in a conventional and orderly fashion, she was convicted in the Mayor's Court and fined ten dollars. She appealed her conviction, arguing that the ordinance was unconstitutional. The Court agreed. "The authors of the First Amendment knew that novel and unconventional ideas might disturb the complacent, but they chose to encourage a freedom which they believed essential if vigorous enlightenment was ever to triumph over slothful ignorance."[3] While this freedom embraces the right to distribute literature, it also "*necessarily protects the right to receive it.*"[4] [emphasis added].

In this case, the Court weighed three interests against each other:

- Ms. Martin's interest in distributing information;
- residents' interest in choosing whether to receive that information; and
- the city's interest in protecting its citizens, whether they want that protection or not.

The Court viewed the city's interest in this ordinance as involving the substitution of its judgment for the judgment of the individual resident. Ms. Martin was convicted of a crime for annoying people on whom she called, even though some of those residents were in fact glad to receive her flyers.[5]

The Court also noted that the city could find a less intrusive means to accomplish the ordinance's purpose, one that would protect the rights of those desiring to distribute literature, those wishing to receive it, and those who wish to exclude such distribution from their homes.[6] In the Court's words: "Freedom to distribute information to every citizen wherever he desires to receive it is so clearly vital to the preservation of a free society that, putting aside reasonable police and health regulations of time and manner of distribution, it must be fully preserved."[7] The dangers the ordinance wished to avoid can easily be controlled by other legal methods. In this way each householder can have the full right to decide whether he or she will receive strangers as visitors. As it stands the current prohibition of the ordinance serves no purpose "but that forbidden by the Constitution, the naked restriction of the dissemination of ideas."[8]

May 1965

In *Lamont* v. *Postmaster General*[9] the Court considered the constitutionality of a federal law that required pieces of mail judged to be communist political propaganda to be held until the addressee is notified. The addressee must then request its receipt in writing before it can be delivered. The question the Court asked was whether this is an unconstitutional abridgment of the addressee's (as opposed to the sender's) First Amendment rights.

The case arose out of the Post Office's detention in 1963 of the *Peking Review #12* addressed to Dr. Corliss Lamont. Instead of responding to the notice of detention, Lamont instituted a suit to enjoin enforcement of the law—the Postal Service and Federal Employees Salary Act of 1962. The Court concluded that "the Act as construed and applied is unconstitutional because it requires an official act (viz., returning the reply card) as a limitation on the unfettered exercise of the addressee's First Amendment rights."[10]

The Court reasoned that the requirement is almost certain to have a deterrent effect on the First Amendment rights of the addressees. Anyone is likely to feel some inhibition in sending for literature that federal officials have condemned as "communist political propaganda. The regime of this Act is therefore at war with the uninhibited, robust, and wide open debate and discussion that are contemplated by the First Amendment."[11]

In a concurring opinion, Justice Brennan pointed out that, in this case, it is not the sender's right to distribute that is being considered, but rather the addressee's claim. Justice Brennan stated that because this case upholds *Martin* (supra), he joins the Court's decision. Government is powerless to interfere with the delivery of this material because the First Amendment necessarily protects the right to receive it. While the First Amendment does not specifically guarantee access to publications, the Bill of Rights protects from congressional abridgment other equally fundamental personal rights necessary to make the express guarantees fully meaningful.[12] Without the right to receive publications, the right to freedom of speech is meaningless. After all, concluded Justice Brennan: "The dissemination of ideas can accomplish nothing if otherwise willing addressees are not free to receive and consider them. *It would be a barren marketplace of ideas that only had sellers and no buyers*."[13] [emphasis added].

June 1965

In *Griswold* v. *Connecticut*[14] the Court followed the precedent set by the two previous cases. Dr. Griswold was the executive director of the Planned Parenthood League of Connecticut, and Dr. Buxton served as the medical director for the league at its center in New Haven, Connecticut. Both doctors gave information, instruction, and medical advice to married persons concerning means of preventing conception. Such advice was prohibited under Connecticut law. The Court ruled the statute unconstitutional on several grounds. Citing *Martin*, the Court declared that "the State may not consistent with the spirit of the First Amendment, contract the spectrum of available knowledge."[15] Freedom of speech and press "includes not only the right to utter or to print, but the right to distribute, the right to receive, the right to read . . . and freedom of inquiry, freedom of thought, and freedom to teach. . . . Without those peripheral rights the specific rights would be less secure."[16]

April 1969

In *Stanley* v. *Georgia*[17] the Court addressed another important question. If the state may protect the body of a citizen, may it not also protect the mind?

While executing a search warrant for evidence of bookmaking, federal and state agents found and seized three obscene films. Mr. Stanley was then arrested and indicted for the knowing possession of obscene matter in violation of Georgia law. Stanley objected on the ground that the statute was unconstitutional because it punishes mere private possession of obscene matter. Citing *Martin, Griswold,* and *Lamont* (supra), the Court stated: "It is now well established that the Constitution protects the right to receive information and ideas."[18]

The Court reasoned that this right, regardless of the information's social worth, is fundamental to a free society. Along with the right to read or observe what a citizen pleases, there is the right "to satisfy his intellectual and emotional needs in the privacy of his own home."[19] A state may no more prohibit mere possession of obscene material on the ground that it may lead to antisocial conduct than it may prohibit possession of chemistry books on the ground that they may lead to the manufacture of homemade spirits.[20] Neither the states nor Congress can constitutionally premise legislation on the desirability of controlling a person's private thoughts.[21]

To the state's assertion that it has the right to protect an individual's mind from the effects of obscenity, the Court replied: "We are not certain that this argument amounts to anything more than the assertion that the State has the right to control the moral content of a person's thoughts."[22] While this may be a noble purpose, it is wholly inconsistent with the philosophy of the First Amendment in this instance.[23]

1969

In *Red Lion Broadcasting Co. v. Federal Communications Commission*[24] the Court extended the right to receive information to a commercial institution, the broadcasting industry. Under the FCC fairness doctrine, when a personal attack was made in the context of controversial public issues, the broadcast licensee was required to notify the individual or group mentioned and offer a reasonable opportunity to respond over the air. Broadcasters challenged this rule on First Amendment grounds. They argued that the First Amendment protects their desire to use their allocated frequencies in whatever way they chose and to exclude whomever they chose from using their frequencies.

The Court ruled that the federal government may limit the use of broadcast equipment, and that the right of free speech does not embrace a right to snuff out the free speech of others. There is nothing in the First Amendment that prevents the federal government from requiring licensees to share their frequencies with others. "It is the right of viewers and listeners, not the right of the broadcasters, which is paramount."[25]

The purpose of the First Amendment is to preserve an uninhibited marketplace of ideas, not to approve a monopolization of the marketplace. "It is the right of the public to receive suitable access to social, political, aesthetic, moral, and other ideas and experiences which is crucial here."[26]

1972

In *Kleindienst* v. *Mandel*[27] the Court set a limit on the right to receive information. This case considered the question of whether the refusal to allow an alien scholar to enter the United States to attend academic meetings violates the First Amendment rights of American scholars and students who wish to hear, speak with, and debate with him. Ernest E. Mandel, a Belgian citizen and editor of the Belgian Left Socialist weekly *La Gauche*, had been invited by the Graduate Student Association at Stanford University to participate in a conference. Mandel had been found ineligible for admission under the Immigration and Nationality Act, which barred those who advocated doctrines of world communism. The attorney general declined to waive Mandel's ineligibility. Mandel and eight university professors who were United States citizens instituted an action to compel the attorney general to allow Mandel's admission to the United States so that he could speak at universities and participate in colloquia. Their action contended that the concern of the First Amendment was not with Mandel's interest in entering and being heard but with the citizens in hearing Mandel explain and defend his views.

Citing *Martin, Lamont, Stanley, Red Lion*, and *Keyishian*, the Court acknowledged that in a variety of contexts it had recognized a First Amendment right to receive information and ideas.[28] However, the Court also noted that, without exception, it had sustained Congress's power to make rules for the admission of aliens or to prescribe the terms and conditions under which aliens came to the United States. The Court reasoned that if the First Amendment argument prevailed whenever a bona fide claim is made by American citizens wishing to meet and talk with excluded aliens, Congress's authority would be a nullity or the Court would be required to weigh the strength of the audience's interest against that of the government in refusing a waiver. The dangers and undesirability of making that determination seem obvious and the

Court upheld Congress's authority to exclude Mandel over the constitutional right to receive ideas and information.

1978

In *First National Bank of Boston* v. *Bellotti*[29]the Court considered whether speech that would otherwise be protected by the First Amendment loses that protection when its source is a corporation. The case involved a challenge to a Massachusetts criminal statute prohibiting banks and business corporations from making contributions or expenditures to influence votes on referendum proposals. The First National Bank of Boston wished to spend money to publicize its views on a proposed constitutional amendment that dealt with a graduated income tax on individuals.

The bank argued that the statute violated the First Amendment. The Court agreed, noting that the First Amendment goes beyond protection of the press and individual self-expression. The First Amendment prohibits government from limiting the stock of information from which members of the public may draw. "A commercial advertisement is constitutionally protected not so much because it pertains to the seller's business as because it furthers the societal interest in the 'free flow of commercial information.'"[30] Citing *Stanley* and *Red Lion* (supra), the Court concluded that such commercial speech affords the public "access to discussion, debate, and the dissemination of information and ideas"[31] when it deals with public debate over controversial interests. Legislatures are thus disqualified from dictating the subjects and the speakers who may address a public issue.[32] For "[i]f a legislature may direct business corporations to 'stick to business,' it may also limit other corporations—religious, charitable, or civic—to their respective 'business' when addressing the public."[33]

1982

In *Board of Education* v. *Pico*[34] (cited hereafter as *Pico*) the Court considered the constitutional right to receive information and ideas as it relates to the censorship of school library books. This was the first school library censorship case decided by the Court.[35] The question presented was whether the First Amendment imposes limitations upon the exercise by a local school board of its discretion to remove library books from high school and junior high school libraries. In February 1976, the Board of Education of the Island Trees Union Free School District No. 26, in New York State, gave an "unofficial direction" that nine books in the high school library and one book in the junior high school library were to be removed from library shelves and delivered to the board's office so that board members could read them.

A press release from the board characterized the books as "anti-American, anti-Christian, anti-Sem[i]tic, and just plain filthy."[36] The release concluded: "[i]t is our duty, our moral obligation, to protect the children in our schools from this moral danger as surely as from physical and medical dangers."[37] The Board appointed a book review committee a short time later to read the books and to recommend to the board whether the books should be retained. In July, the committee made its final report, recommending that five of the books be retained and that two others be removed from the school libraries. The Committee was divided on the remaining books. The board subsequently rejected the committee's report and decided that only one book should be returned to the high school library and that another should be made available subject to parental consent. The board gave no reason for rejecting the recommendations of the committee it appointed.

A group of students brought a suit in U.S. District Court claiming that the board's actions denied them their rights under the First Amendment. They asked for a declaration that the board's actions were unconstitutional and for an injunction ordering the board to return the books to the school libraries. The District Court substantially agreed with the board's motivation, reasoning that: "The board has restricted access only to certain books which the board believed to be, in essence, vulgar. While removal of such books from a school library may . . . reflect a misguided educational philosophy, it does not constitute a sharp and direct infringement of any First Amendment right."[38]

The U.S. Court of Appeals reversed the District Court decision. The U.S. Supreme Court then agreed to hear the case. (See Appendix A for the text of the Court's majority opinion.) The Court began by noting that the only books at issue in this case are library books, which are not required as part of the school's curriculum, and that this issue does not involve the acquisition of new books for the library. The students were not trying to compel the board to add to the school library shelves any books that students desire to read. The only action being challenged was the removal from the school libraries of books originally placed there by the school authorities, or at least without objections from them.[39]

The Court's reasoning began by noting that the Court had long recognized that local school boards have broad discretion in the management of school affairs. However, the discretion of these local and state boards must comport with the "transcendent imperatives of the First Amendment."[40] Boards of education are educating the young for citizenship. If the boards do not scrupulously protect the constitutional freedoms of individuals they "strangle the free mind at its source and teach youth to discount important principles of our government as mere platitudes."[41] First Amendment rights are thus available to students.

The Court noted that courts in general should not intervene in the daily operation of school systems unless basic constitutional values are directly and sharply implicated. In this case, because of the right of students to receive information and ideas, the Court must intervene. In the opinion of the Court, the First Amendment rights of students are directly and sharply limited by the removal of books from the shelves of a school library.

Citing *First National Bank, Griswold, Stanley, Struthers*, and *Lamont* (supra) the Court reasoned that the First Amendment affords the public access to discussion, debate, and the dissemination of information and ideas. The right to receive information and ideas is an inherent corollary of the rights of free speech and press in two senses. First, the right to receive ideas "follows ineluctably from the *sender's* First Amendment right" to send them. *Martin* stated that the right of freedom of speech and press protects the right to receive what is spoken and what is written. The dissemination of ideas cannot accomplish anything if willing addressees are not free to receive and consider them. As Justice Brennan stated in *Lamont* (supra): it would be a barren marketplace of ideas that had only sellers and no buyers. But more importantly, "the right to receive ideas is a necessary predicate to the *recipient's* meaningful exercise of his own rights of speech, press, and political freedom."[42]

In short, just as access to ideas enables citizens to meaningfully exercise their rights of free speech and press, such access also prepares students for active and effective participation in the pluralistic, often contentious society of which they will soon be adult members. Of course, the First Amendment rights of students must be viewed in the school environment.

> But the special characteristics of the school *library* make that environment especially appropriate for the recognition of the First Amendment rights of students.
>
> A school library, no less than any other public library, is "a place dedicated to quiet, to knowledge, and to beauty." *Brown* v. *Louisiana*, 383 U.S. 131, 142 (1966)(opinion of Fortas, J.). *Keyishian* v. *Board of Regents*, 385 U.S. 589 (1967), observed that "'students must always remain free to inquire, to study and to evaluate, to gain new maturity

and understanding.'" The school library is the principal locus of such freedom.[43]

Quoting a district court opinion, the Court noted that in a school library "a student can literally explore the unknown, and discover areas of interest and thought not covered by the prescribed curriculum. . . . Th[e] student learns that a library is a place to test or expand upon ideas presented to him, in or out of the classroom." The board emphasizes that it must be allowed *unfettered* discretion to transmit community values. This claim, however, overlooks the unique role of the school library.

> It appears from the record that the use of the Island Trees school libraries is completely voluntary on the part of students. Their selection of books from these libraries is entirely a matter of free choice; the libraries afford them an opportunity at self-education and individual enrichment that is wholly optional.[44]

The board's reliance upon its claim of absolute discretion beyond the compulsory environment of the classroom is misplaced in "the school library and the regime of voluntary inquiry that there holds sway."[45]

To what extent then does the First Amendment place limitations on the board's discretion to remove books from its libraries? The Court noted that while the board has significant discretion in determining the content of its school library, that discretion may not be exercised in a narrowly political manner. "If a Democratic school board, motivated by party affiliation, ordered the removal of all books written by or in favor of Republicans, few would doubt that the order violated the constitutional rights of the students denied access to those books."[46] The Constitution "does not permit the official suppression of *ideas*."[47] If the board *intended* to deny students access to ideas with which it disagreed, and such disagreement was a decisive factor in its decision, then the board exercised its discretion in violation of the Constitution. If the books were removed based solely upon the educational suitability, then the removal would be permissible.

The Court then looked at the case's particulars to determine if there was evidence of the motivation behind the board's removal decision. The Court noted that there was no record of an established, regular, and facially unbiased procedure for review of controversial materials. In fact, quite the opposite was true. The board had indeed ignored the views of librarians, teachers, the superintendent of schools, and the "guidance of publications that rate books for junior and senior high school students."[48] Based on the evidence, the board's removal decision seems highly irregular and ad hoc. The Court then ordered the case back to the lower courts to determine the board's actual motivation.

There were four dissenting decisions in this case. While none contested the right to receive information, the dissenters argued that the students could not freely exercise this right in the public school setting. Justice Rehnquist noted that the libraries of elementary and secondary schools serve a different purpose than other libraries. "Unlike universities or public libraries, elementary and secondary schools are not designed for freewheeling inquiry; they are tailored, to teaching of basic skills and ideas."[49]

LIBRARIES AND THE RIGHT TO INFORMATION

Access to Libraries

In 1992, the United States Court of Appeals for the Third Circuit considered the constitutional right of access to information and ideas in relation to the public's right of access to libraries. The case[50] dealt with a public library's authority to promulgate and enforce regulations governing the use of its facilities. A homeless man, Richard R. Kreimer, was expelled from the Joint Free Public Library of Morristown and Morris Township for violating rules governing patron conduct. Kreimer filed suit in the the United States District Court of New Jersey alleging that the library rules were facially invalid under the First and Fourteenth Amendments. The district court accepted Kreimer's arguments and issued a summary judgment declaring that the library rules were indeed facially unconstitutional. An injunction was then issued.

Kreimer based his First Amendment claim on the constitutional right to receive information and ideas. In his brief, he cited the "vital role played by public libraries" in promoting the fullest exercise of that right. After reviewing *Martin, Lamont, Griswold, Stanley, Red Lion Broadcasting,* and *Pico,* the court of appeals agreed that the constitutional right to receive information was implicated in this case and there was thus a First Amendment right to "some level of access to a public library."[51] Like other First Amendment rights, however, the right to receive information is not "unfettered and may give way to significant countervailing interests."[52] For instance, time, manner, and place restrictions can be reasonable.

In this case, the circuit court found that the library's rules were reasonable "manner" restrictions.[53] The library's interest in achieving the optimum and best use of its facilities warranted restricting patrons' access to the library. Libraries are in general places dedicated to quiet, knowledge, and to beauty.[54] This library was established as a place to aid the acquisition of knowledge through reading, writing, and quiet contemplation. The exercise of other more verbal interactive First Amendment activities is antithetical to the nature of the library.[55]

In short, the Third Circuit held in this case that a library is a public forum, but it is a limited public forum. It is limited to those activities that are consistent with the nature of a library as a place of study. These types of activities are protected by the First Amendment, but the library may legimately regulate other activities.

Kreimer was not appealed to the Supreme Court but has been cited as precedent in several non-library cases in the Third Circuit. Some of the issues raised in the case have also been noted by courts in other circuits, but none has dealt with the constitutional right of access to a library.

Kreimer also raised other constitutional issues—due process and equal protection—related to library access. These are discussed in Chapter 4. The relationship between the the constitutional right to receive information and to privacy, especially in library records, is examined in Chapter 5.

ENDNOTES

1. *Kreimer* v. *Bureau of Police for Town of Morristown*, 958 F.2d 1242 at 1255 (1992).
2. 319 U.S. 141.
3. Ibid. at 143.
4. Ibid.
5. Ibid. at 145. "While door to door distributors of literature may be either a nuisance or a blind for criminal activities, they may also be useful members of society engaged in the dissemination of ideas in accordance with the best tradition of free discussion."
6. Ibid. at 146–147.
7. Ibid.
8. Ibid.
9. 381 U.S. 301.
10. Ibid. at 305.
11. Ibid. at 307.
12. Ibid. at 308.
13. Ibid.
14. 381 U.S. 479.

15. Ibid. at 482–483.
16. Ibid.
17. 394 U.S. 557.
18. Ibid. at 564.
19. Ibid. at 565.
20. Ibid. at 567.
21. Ibid. at 566.
22. Ibid. at 565.
23. See also *Osborne* v. *Ohio*, 495 U.S. 103 (1990).
24. 395 U.S. 369.
25. Ibid. at 390.
26. Ibid.
27. 408 U.S. 753.
28. Ibid. at 762.
29. 435 U.S. 765.
30. Ibid. at 783.
31. Ibid. at 783.
32. Ibid. at 786.
33. Ibid. at 785.
34. 457 U.S. 853.
35. To date, the Court has not directly decided a public library censorship case.
36. Ibid. at 857.
37. 474 F.Supp. 387 at 390 (1979).
38. Ibid. at 397.
39. *Pico* at 862.
40. Ibid. at 864.
41. *West Virginia Board of Education* v. *Barnette*, 319 U.S. 624 at 637 (1943).
42. *Pico* at 867–868.
43. Ibid. at 868–869.
44. Ibid at 869.
45. Ibid.
46. Ibid. at 871.
47. Ibid.
48. Ibid. at 874.
49. Ibid. at 915.
50. *Kreimer* at 1246.
51. Ibid. at 1251.
52. Ibid.
53. Ibid. at 1246.
54. *Brown* v. *Louisiana*, 383 U.S. 131 at 142 (1966).
55. *Kreimer* at 1261.

4
Forum, Due Process, and Equal Protection

- *Does everyone have a constitutional right to use a public library?*
- *Is a rule requiring library patrons to be engaged in library activities or face ejection a reasonable one?*
- *Does this constitutional right of access apply to patrons with offensive bodily hygiene?*
- *How can library rules comply with the due process and equal protection provisions of the Fourteenth Amendment?*

An inquiry into the legal rights of library patrons must begin with the question of access. If the use of a library is only a privilege, then access can be denied for any reason. If, however, the right to use a library is grounded in the Constitution, then a higher standard of cause is required.

Private Libraries

The Constitution generally affects the rights of citizens only in their relationship to their government—not as they relate to private institutions. Thus, a constitutional right of access does not generally apply to a privately funded and managed library that receives no government funding or benefit. Such libraries are generally free to determine who can use their facilities. Receiving some government benefits, however, does obligate a library to some level of public access. A library, for example, that is designed as a federal depository must make its government documents available to the public, no matter what its source of funding.[1] Private libraries that make their collections available to researchers outside of their organizations have access to some of the special copyright privileges granted libraries under section 108 of the Copyright Law of 1976. Many states also offer similar incentives to libraries that open their doors at least partway to the general public.

First Amendment

The right of access to a public library lies principally in the Speech Clause of the First Amendment. The clause declares that "Congress shall make no laws . . . abridging the freedom of speech, or of the press. . . ." The right to receive information and ideas is founded under this. The right to receive information and ideas is so essential to the purposes and functions of the Speech Clause of the First Amendment that it must be considered a part of the amendment although the right is not actually mentioned in the words of the clause.

Fourteenth Amendment

The First Amendment is made applicable to states, local governments, and municipal agencies like public libraries though the Fourteenth Amendment. The Due Process Clause of the Fourteenth Amendment declares that "No State shall make or enforce any law which shall abridge the privileges or immunities of citizens of the United States; *nor shall any State* deprive any person of life, *liberty*, or property, without due process of law; nor deny to any person within its jurisdiction the *equal protection* of the laws." [emphasis added]. In 1925 the Court ruled that freedom of speech is among the "liberties" that no citizen can be deprived of by any state or its subdivisions without due process of law.[2] In addition, the states cannot deny any person within their boundaries of the equal protection of the law.

FORUM

In 1992, the Third Circuit Court of Appeals ruled in the case of *Kreimer* v. *Bureau of Police for Town of Morristown* that the constitutional right to ideas and information "includes the right to some level of access to a public library. . . ."[3] The court made this determination because it saw libraries as the "quintessential locus of the receipt of information."[4] While the circuit court's decision is binding only on the courts in the Third Circuit, the decision is persuasive to courts in other jurisdictions.

The recognition that the constitutional right protecting public access to information and ideas applies to the public library is, however, only the beginning of our inquiry. We must determine, as the Third Circuit did, what type of forum a public library is for the purpose of speech. The extent to which the library may limit access really "depends on whether the forum is public or nonpublic."[5]

First Cases

The fact that property is owned by government does not automatically open that property to the public.[6] The earliest decision of the Court, in fact, did not distinguish public property from private when it came to the Free Speech Clause. In 1897, the Court ruled that the Massachusetts legislature could forbid public speeches in public parks the same way owners of a private home could prohibit them in their own house.[7] It was not until 1939 that the Court began to protect speech rights on public property. Justice Roberts, in a majority opinion, said:

> Wherever the title of streets and parks may rest, they have immemorially been held in trust for purposes of assembly, communicating thoughts between citizens, and discussing public questions. Such use of the streets and public places has, from ancient times, been part of the privileges, immunities, rights, and liberties of citizens.[8]

Like the First Amendment itself, the right of speech in public places was not in the Court's view absolute. Justice Roberts wrote:

> The privilege of a citizen of the United States to use the streets and parks for communication of views on national questions may be regulated in the interest of all; it is not absolute, but relative, and must be exercised in subordination to the general comfort and convenience, and in consonance with peace and good order; but it must not, in the guise of regulation, be abridged or denied.[9]

Following this decision, the Court has developed two positions on the issue of forum.

Incompatibility Test

The first position is known as the incompatibility test. It first appeared in a 1972 case involving a public protest on a sidewalk about 100 feet from a public high school to demand equal rights for black students. The question before the Court was whether a local ordinance unduly interfered with First and Fourteenth Amendment rights to picket on a public sidewalk near a school.

Following the reasoning advanced by Justice Roberts in the 1897 case, the Court concluded that a city could reasonably regulate speech activities on public property if the regulation advanced a significant government interest.[10] The right to use a public place for expressive activity may be restricted only for weighty reasons. While government has no right to restrict such activity because of its message, it does, however, have the right to make reasonable time, place, and manner regulations. For example, two organizations cannot march on the same street simultaneously. The city has the right to allow only one.

The Court developed a test for determining whether restrictions on speech in public places constituted reasonable time, place, or manner limitations. The test involved determining whether "the manner of expression is basically incompatible with the normal activity of a particular place at a particular time."[11] The Court reasoned that the "nature of a place, the pattern of its normal activities, dictate the kinds of regulations of time, place and manner that are reasonable."[12] The Court noted that while a silent vigil may not unduly interfere with a public library, making a speech in the reading room almost certainly would. That same speech, however, would be perfectly appropriate in a park.[13]

Under this incompatibility test, the Court analyzes the nature of the forum to determine "when the Government's interest in limiting the use of its property to its intended purpose outweighs the interest of those wishing to use the property for other purposes."[14] In other words, the extent to which government can limit access for speech activities depends on the nature of the forum. To determine if a forum is open to the public for speech activities, the courts balance the interests of the speakers against the need for government to operate in an efficient way. If these are incompatible, then speech activity is prohibited.

Perry

The second approach was named after the case in which it first appeared. In *Perry Education Assn.* v. *Perry Local Educators' Association*,[15] the Court announced three categories of forum for determining how speech interests on government property are to be determined.

The first category is places such as streets and parks. These places have always been used by the public for gathering, talking, and debating public issues. In these places, which by long tradition or by explicit government action have been devoted to assembly and debate, the state's right to limit speech activities is sharply circumscribed. Here, government cannot prohibit all speech activities.[16] In these places government can regulate only the time, place, and manner of speech. It cannot limit the content. These regulations must also be narrowly written to serve only a significant government interest, and they must leave open ample alternative channels. This category is known as a "traditional public forum."

The second category includes places such as school board meetings, university meeting facilities, or municipal theaters. This public property is opened by government for use by the public as a place for expressive activities. States are prohibited from placing certain limitations on a place generally open to the public even if government was not required to create the place for speech activities in the first place.[17] Although government is not required to indefinitely retain the open character of the place, as long as it does, it is bound by the same standards as the first category, the traditional public forum. Reasonable time, place, and manner regulations are permissible, and any content-based prohibition must be narrowly drawn to effectuate a compelling state interest. This category is known as a "designated" or "limited public forum."

The third category is public property that is not by custom or designation a forum for speech activities.[18] The First Amendment does not guarantee access to property just because it is owned or controlled by government. In these places government can make time, place, and manner regulations and may even reserve the place for its intended government use so long as the regulations are reasonable and not an effort to suppress expression merely because public officials oppose the speaker's view. This category is known as a "nonpublic forum."

In short, regulation of speech activity on government property that has been traditionally open to the public for expressive activity, such as public streets and parks, is examined under strict scrutiny.[19] Regulation of speech on property that the government has expressly dedicated to speech activity is also examined under strict scrutiny. But regulation of speech activity where the government has not dedicated its property to First Amendment activity is examined only for reasonableness.

Public Libraries

What type of forum is a public library? In *Kreimer* the Third Circuit Court ruled that a library is clearly not a traditional public forum. A library is obviously not like a public park, sidewalk, or street. A library patron cannot be permitted to give a speech or engage in any conduct that would disrupt the quiet and peaceful library environment.[20] A lower federal court had ruled that a library constituted a "quintessential" traditional public form because its accessibility affects the bedrock of our democratic system.[21] The circuit court rejected this view.

Is the library a designated public forum? At first a library does not seem to fit the second category either. However, in *Kreimer*, the Third Circuit took a hard look at the Court's recent decisions relating to designated public fora since *Perry*. In 1985, the Court considered a case involving the NAACP Legal Defense Fund. The case turned on whether a nontraditional forum is opened for public discourse by inaction or by permitting limited discourse. The Court concluded that it is not. Instead, the Court looked to policy and practice to ascertain whether government actually intended to designate as a public forum a place not traditionally open to assembly and debate. In addition, the Court examined the nature of the place and whether it is compatible with the expressive activity.[22] In this case, the Court found that neither the practice nor the policy of the Legal Defense fund was consistent with the intent to designate the fund as a public forum.

In 1990, the Court considered a case dealing with Postal Service property. In that case, defendants were convicted of soliciting contributions on a sidewalk completely on Postal Service property in front of a post office in violation of Postal Service regulations. The defendants contended that the sidewalk was a public forum and that regulations were not narrowly tailored to further a significant government interest. The Court concluded that the:

> Postal service has not expressly dedicated its sidewalks to any expressive activity. Indeed, postal property is expressly dedicated to only one means of communication: the posting of public notices on designated bulletin boards . . . No postal service regulation opens postal sidewalks to any First Amendment activity.[23]

In short, government does not create a public forum by permitting discourse, but only by intentionally opening a nontraditional forum for public discourse.[24]

What does this mean for libraries? In *Kreimer*, the circuit court identified a subcategory of a designated public forum to describe a public library. According to the court a public library constitutes a limited public forum. Government did intentionally open the library to the public for reading, studying, and using library materials; it did not, however, open the door for the exercise of all First Amendment activities.[25]

In addition, the Third Circuit looked at the nature of a public library to determine what kinds of expressive activities were inconsistent with its nature. The court concluded that a library's purpose is to aid in the acquisition of knowledge through reading, writing, and quiet contemplation. The exercise of other "oral or interactive" First Amendment activities is antithetical to the nature of a library. These conflicting characteristics support the court's conclusion that a library is a limited public forum.[26]

Library Rules

In a limited public forum, government restrictions can only be reasonable time, place, or manner restrictions, and not efforts to suppress expression merely because public officials oppose the speaker's view.[27] In *Kreimer*, the circuit court considered three rules established by the library involved in the suit. Rule 1 was:

> Patrons shall be engaged in activities associated with the use of a public library while in the building. Patrons not engaged in reading, studying, or using library materials shall be required to leave the building.[28]

The circuit court determined that this rule is reasonable and is "perfectly valid."[29] The purpose behind the rule is to foster a quiet and orderly atmosphere. Such an atmosphere is conducive to every patron's exercise of his or her constitutionally protected interest in written communications. Requiring library patrons to make use of the library in order to be permitted to remain is reasonably related to the purpose of the library as a limited public forum for access to ideas.

Rule 5 stated:

> Patrons shall respect the rights of other patrons and shall not harass or annoy others through noisy or boisterous activities, by staring at another person with the intent to annoy that person, by following another person about the building with the intent to annoy that person, by playing audio equipment so that others can hear it, by singing or talking loudly to others or in monologues, or by behaving in a manner which reasonably can be expected to disturb other patrons.

The circuit court also found this rule to be reasonable and rejected any attack on it. Rule 5 prohibits behavior that tends to be or is disruptive in a library setting. Prohibiting such disruptive behavior is, in the court's opinion, the clearest and most direct way to achieve maximum library use.[30]

Rule 9 stated in part:

> Patrons whose bodily hygiene is offensive so as to constitute a nuisance to other persons shall be required to leave the building.[31]

This rule is also reasonable, although it might require the expulsion of a patron who might be peacefully engaged in library activities. The court reasoned that the library has a significant interest in ensuring that all patrons use the library to the maximum extent possible during its regularly scheduled hours. The rule furthers that significant interest because it prohibits one patron from unreasonably interfering with other patrons' use and enjoyment of the library. In addition, this rule leaves open alternative channels. So long as the patron complies with the rules, he or she may use the library's facilities. In addition, although the library may eject a patron for violating this rule, a patron may reenter the library once he or she complies with the requirements.[32]

The circuit court did concede that Rule 9 disproportionately affects the homeless, who have limited bathing facilities. This concession would not, however, justify permitting a would-be patron's offensive hygiene to force other patrons to leave the library or inhibit library employees from performing their duties. Although the First Amendment protects the right to reasonable access to a public library, this right cannot be expanded so that it denies others the same guarantee.

DUE PROCESS

Vagueness

The Fourteenth Amendment requires that no citizen be deprived of liberty without due process of law. One of the due process challenges to library rules involves the "void-for-vagueness" doctrine. This doctrine was originally used to invalidate penal statutes that did not define a criminal offense with sufficient definiteness so that an ordinary person could understand what behavior is being prohibited. A vagueness challenge to a library rule will succeed if a patron does not have actual notice of what activity is prohibited. The vagueness doctrine seeks to ensure fair and nondiscriminatory application of rules. It finds repulsive rules that endow officials with undue discretion to determine whether a certain activity violates a library rule. Fair notice and fair enforcement of library rules is needed to avoid a vagueness challenge.[33]

In the case of the library rules considered in *Kreimer*, library patrons should not be immediately expelled but informed first that they must use library materials if they are to remain in the library. Rule 5 is not vague because it lists specific behavior that is deemed annoying to others and does not require a subjective determination. In the case of Rule 9, the determination of whether a person's hygiene constitutes a nuisance involves an objective reasonableness test.[34] It is a nuisance when it substantially interferes with others' rights.

Arbitrary and Discriminatory

These rules do not make personal attributes such as appearance, smell, and manner of cleanliness determinative factors in enforcement of the library rules. The rules are not arbitrary. They were not adopted without cause, justification, or reason.

EQUAL PROTECTION

The Fourteenth Amendment prohibits a state from denying to any person within its jurisdiction the *equal protection* of the laws. In the case of the rules in *Kreimer*, the equal protection would be denied library patrons if the library enacted the rules with the explicit intention of restricting homeless persons' access to the library. The record indicates that the library enacted these rules to provide a fair method to expel any disruptive patron in order to optimize library usage.[35]

ENDNOTES

1. 44 USC Sec. 1911. "Depository libraries shall make Government publications available for the free use of the general public. . . ."
2. "For present purposes we may and do assume that freedom of speech and of the press—which are protected by the First Amendment from abridgment by Congress—are among the fundamental personal rights and 'liberties' protected by the due process clause of the Fourteenth Amendment from impairment by the States." *Gitlow* v. *New York*, 268 U.S. 652 at 666 (1925).

3. 958 F.2d 1242 at 1255.
4. Ibid.
5. *Cornelius* v. *NAACP Legal Defense & Educational Fund, Inc.*, 473 U.S. 788 at 797 (1985).
6. *United States Postal Service* v. *Council of Greenburgh Civic Associations*, 453 U.S. 114 at 129 (1981).
7. *Davis* v. *Massachusetts*, 167 U.S. 43 at 47–48.
8. *Hague* v. *CIO*, 307 U.S. 496 at 515.
9. Ibid., at 515–516.
10. *Grayned* v. *City of Rockford*, 408 U.S. 104 at 115.
11. Ibid. at 116.
12. Ibid.
13. Ibid.
14. *Cornelius* v. *NAACP Legal Defense and Educational Fund*, 473 U. S. 788 at 800.
15. 460 U.S. 37 (1983).
16. Ibid. In the Court's words:

In places which, by long tradition or by government fiat, have been devoted to assembly and debate, the rights of the State to limit expressive activity are sharply circumscribed. At one end of the spectrum are streets and parks, which have immemorially been held in trust for the use of the public and, time out of mind, have been used for purposes of assembly, communicating thoughts between citizens, and discussing public questions. . . .In these quintessential public forums, the government may not prohibit all communicative activity. For the State to enforce a content-based exclusion, it must show that its regulation is necessary to serve a compelling state interest and that it is narrowly drawn to achieve that end. . . . The State may also enforce regulations of the time, place, and manner of expression which are content-neutral, are narrowly tailored to serve a significant government interest, and leave open ample alternative channels of communication.

17. Ibid. In the Court's words:

A second category consists of public property which the State has opened for use by the public as a place for expressive activity. The Constitution forbids a State to enforce certain exclusions from a forum generally open to the public even if it was not required to create the forum in the first place. . . . Although a State is not required to indefinitely retain the open character of the facility, as long as it does so, it is bound by the same standards as apply in a traditional public forum. Reasonable time, place, and manner regulations are permissible, and a content-based prohibition must be narrowly drawn to effectuate a compelling state interest.

18. Ibid. In the Court's words:

Public property which is not, by tradition or designation, a forum for public communication is governed by different standards. We have recognized that the "First Amendment does not guarantee access to property simply because it is owned or controlled by the government." . . . In addition to time, place, and manner regulations, the State may reserve the forum for its intended purposes, communicative or otherwise, as long as the regulation on speech is reasonable and not an effort to suppress expression merely because public officials oppose the speaker's view. . . .

19. Ibid. at 45.
20. *Kreimer v. Bureau of Police for Town of Morristown*, 958 F.2d 1242 at 1256 (1992).
21. 765 F. Supp. at 181.
22. *Cornelius v. NAACP Legal Defense & Educational Fund, Inc.*, 473 U.S. 788 at 802.
23. *United States v. Kokinda*, 497 U.S. 720 at 726.
24. Ibid.
25. *Kreimer*, at 1260.
26. Ibid., at 1261.
27. *Kokinda*, at 802.
28. *Kreimer*, at 1262.
29. Ibid.
30. Ibid., at 1262–1263.
31. Ibid., at 1264.
32. Ibid.
33. Ibid., at 1266–1267.
34. Ibid., at 1268.
35. Ibid. at 1269.

5

Right to Privacy

- *What is the relationship between the First Amendment and the constitutional right to privacy?*
- *Under what provisions of the Constitution is the right to privacy guaranteed?*
- *Does this constitutional right to privacy protect the confidentiality of library records?*

Patrons take it for granted that their library records are confidential; people use libraries to make some of the most personal and intimate decisions in their lives. Such research should not be made public. The privacy of library records thus raises important constitutional issues.

The Constitution does not explicitly establish a right to privacy. Yet the Court, in interpreting that Constitution, has recognized for over a hundred years that a right to personal privacy exists.[1] In this chapter the constitutional right to privacy is carefully examined to determine what protection it offers to the confidentiality of library records. We begin by analyzing the Court's recognition of the constitutional right to privacy. The role of that right in the disclosure of personal records held by government is then considered.

DEFINITION

Privacy is a broad, abstract, and somewhat ambiguous concept[2] for which the Court has not yet delineated any comprehensive definition. In 1928, Justice Brandeis referred to privacy as simply the "right to be let alone"[3] and almost forty years later the same words were still being used by the Court.[4] Since the Constitution defines the rights of citizens only as they relate to government (not as they relate to each other), privacy in this sense means the right to be free of unjustifiable intrusion by government upon the individual. The Court has seen this as involving two distinct interests:

1. The individual's interest in avoiding disclosure of personal matters by the government. We can call this "disclosural" privacy.[5]
2. The interest in independence from government in making certain decisions in such personal areas as family, travel, and education.[6] This we will call "autonomy."[7]

Like other constitutional rights, the right to privacy is part of the concept of liberty and the pursuit of happiness described in the Declaration of Independence as an inalienable right.[8] It is a fundamental right[9] that is deep-rooted in our society.[10] It is also a right that the Court has speculated existed long before the Bill of Rights.[11]

SOURCES

The word *privacy* is not used in the Constitution or Bill of Rights, and the right to privacy cannot be inferred from any single amendment. One member of the Court, Justice Black, doubted that a general constitutional right to privacy could be found in the Constitution.[12] On the other hand, Justice Douglas felt that it emanated from the totality of the constitutional scheme.[13] The roots of the right to privacy, however, have been generally seen by the Court to lie in the guarantees of rights in several amendments and in their penumbras. These guarantees create constitutional zones of privacy into which government may not intrude.

First Amendment

One of these roots is the First Amendment. As we have seen in Chapter 1, the First Amendment has penumbral rights that, while not specifically mentioned in its clauses, are essential to the full exercise of the rights that are enumerated in the amendment. The Court has acknowledged that the First Amendment includes the penumbral rights to:

- educate a child in a school of its parents' choice;[14]
- study any particular subject or any foreign language;[15]

- read;[16]
- inquire, think, or teach;[17]
- receive information and ideas (see Chapter 2).

The First Amendment right to freedom of association also derives from the amendment's periphery or penumbra.

The right of association was first enunciated by the Court in 1958. The case involved the right of the National Association for the Advancement of Colored People to keep its membership list private. The Court reasoned that the full exercise of freedom of speech includes the freedom to engage in association for the advancement of beliefs and ideas.[18] If an association like the NAACP were required by law to reveal the names and addresses of its membership, that compelled disclosure could result in a substantial restraint on the members' personal freedom to associate. In the case of groups with dissenting views, such disclosure might expose its members to threats, loss of employment, and public hostility. It could result in members withdrawing from the association and dissuading others from joining it because of fear of exposure of their beliefs.[19] In short, the First Amendment must protect association members' privacy from government intrusion if the rights explicitly guaranteed in the First Amendment are to have any functionality at all.

The Court has held that this right of privacy in associations applies to political, social, and legal associations as well as associations formed for the economic benefit of their members.[20] The right also goes beyond limiting disclosure of membership lists. In 1957, the Court held that it is not permissible to bar a lawyer from practicing law because he had once been a member of the Communist Party.[21] Membership in a group must go beyond the right to attend a meeting. It must also include the right to express one's attitudes or philosophies by membership in a group or by affiliation with it. Association is a form of expression of opinion. While not explicitly included in the First Amendment, the right of association is necessary to make the express guarantees of the First Amendment fully meaningful.[22] In other words, the First Amendment has a penumbra that creates a constitutional zone of privacy where government may not intrude,[23] and this is privacy.

Third Amendment

Another root to the constitutional right of privacy is the Third Amendment's prohibition against the quartering of soldiers "in any house" in time of peace without the consent of the owner.[24] Another aspect of freedom from government intrusion, this is the right of civilians to be left alone in their own homes, at least in times of peace. The Third Amendment creates a constitutional zone of privacy in this instance.

Fourth Amendment[25]

The Fourth Amendment explicitly affirms the "right of the people to be secure in their persons, houses, papers, and effects, against unreasonable searches and seizures shall not be violated. . . ." This amendment derives from a 1765 English case[26] that determined that British law did not allow officers of the Crown to break into a citizen's home, under cover of a general assistance writ, to search for evidence of the utterance of libel.[27] English authorities had used these writs in colonial times to enter any house to seize smuggled goods.

In 1961, the Court referred to the Fourth Amendment as creating a "right to privacy, no less important than any other right carefully and particularly reserved to the people."[28] In 1965, the Court interpreted this amendment as creating a constitutional zone of privacy.[29] In 1967, the Court held that the Fourth Amendment protects people, not places. "What a person knowingly exposes to the public even in his own home or office, is not a subject of Fourth Amendment protection. . . . " But what he seeks to preserve as private, even in an area accessible to the public, may be constitutionally protected."[30] This was the source of the Court's current practice of inquiring in criminal search and seizure cases as to whether the defendant had a "reasonable expectation of privacy" in the area where evidence was found by the police.

Fifth Amendment

The Self-Incrimination Clause[31] of the Fifth Amendment also creates a zone of privacy.[32] Government may not force persons to bear witness against themselves, surrendering this zone of privacy to their detriment. The Self-Incrimination Clause was intended to prevent the use of the English *ex officio* oaths. These oaths required defendants to admit their crimes and were used to root out political heresies during the period of the infamous Star Chamber in England.

In an 1886 case, the Court described the Fourth and Fifth Amendments as protection against all governmental invasions of the "sanctity of a man's home and the privacies of life."[33] In 1966, the Court stated that the Fifth Amendment reflects the Constitution's concern for the right of each individual "to a private enclave where he may lead a private life."[34]

Ninth Amendment

Unlike the other earlier amendments in the Bill of Rights, the Ninth Amendment does not enumerate any specific rights. The amendment instead opens the door to other rights not specifically mentioned in the first eight amendments. In a 1965 opinion, Justice Goldberg reasoned that both the language and the history of the Ninth Amendment indicate that the Constitution's framers believed that there are additional fundamental rights that exist alongside those mentioned in the first eight amendments.

The Ninth Amendment states: "The enumeration in the Constitution, of certain rights, shall not be construed to deny or disparage others retained by the people." The Ninth Amendment was introduced by James Madison in order to quiet fears that a bill of specifically enumerated rights would not be broad enough to cover all essential rights. It was also feared that the specific mention of a right would be interpreted as a denial that others are protected.[35]

Justice Goldberg argued that this makes it clear that the first eight amendments were not intended to be construed to exhaust the basic and fundamental rights the Constitution guaranteed. He stated: "To hold that a right so basic and fundamental and so deeply-rooted in our society as the right of privacy in marriage may be infringed because that right is not guaranteed in so many words by the first eight amendments to the Constitution is to ignore the Ninth Amendment and to give it no effect whatsoever."[36]

Fourteenth Amendment[37]

Another root of the constitutional right to privacy is the concept of liberty as it is used in the Fourteenth Amendment. Liberty appears in the first paragraph of the Fourteenth Amendment in the phrase: ". . . nor shall any state deprive any person of life, *liberty*, or property, without due process of law . . ." [emphasis added]. While the Court has not attempted to specifically define the concept of liberty as it is used in this phrase, it has enumerated several rights that are guaranteed by it. The Court stated in 1923 that:

> Without doubt, it [liberty] denotes not merely freedom from bodily restraint, but also the right of the individual to contract, to engage in any of the common occupations of life, *to acquire useful knowledge*, to

marry, establish a home and bring up children, to worship God according to the dictates of his own conscience, and, generally, to enjoy those privileges long recognized at common law as essential to the orderly pursuit of happiness by free men.[38] [emphasis added].

The Fourteenth Amendment protects only these and other rights that are so rooted in the traditions and conscience of the American people as to be considered "fundamental." For example, freedom of thought and speech is a fundamental right because it is the indispensable condition of nearly every form of freedom. With rare exception, such recognition can be found throughout America's political and legal history and is a logical imperative when liberty is more than an exemption from physical restraint. Liberty would not exist if that right were sacrificed.[39] States cannot deprive any person of these liberties arbitrarily or without a reasonable relation to that state's interest—in other words, "without due process" as mentioned in the first paragraph of the Fourteenth Amendment.

Nature of the Right

The right to privacy that gets its life and substance from these various amendments is not, however, absolute. Like the amendments from which it is derived, the constitutional right to privacy has limitations and exceptions. These limitations and exceptions can be seen when the constitutional right to privacy is applied to records kept by government.

GOVERNMENT RECORDS AND THE RIGHT TO PRIVACY

While virtually every government action interferes in some way with personal privacy, the question the courts must ask is whether that government interference violates a right guaranteed by the Constitution.[40] Most of the privacy cases decided by the Court have been concerned with autonomy. Such cases restrict government interference in important individual decisions within the zones of privacy. With a few notable exceptions, the Court has, however, said little about the constitutional dimensions of disclosural privacy.

Marital Relationship

In 1965, the Court decided the case of *Griswold* v. *Connecticut*.[41] The Court's ruling, also discussed in Chapter 3 because of its bearing on the right to receive information, has important implications regarding the right to privacy as well. Dr. Griswold was the executive director and Dr. Buxton the medical director of the Planned Parenthood League Center in New Haven. As part of their duties they prescribed contraceptive devices and materials. Under Connecticut statutes at the time, it was illegal to use contraceptive devices or to assist, abet, or counsel another in their use. Both doctors were found guilty as accessories.

The Court ruled the statute unconstitutional on several grounds. One was that the marital relationship lies within the zone of privacy. The Court reasoned that Connecticut's law forbidding the use of contraceptives attempts to accomplish its goal by means that have the maximum destructive impact on the marital relationship. The law could have just as easily regulated the manufacture or sale of contraceptive devices. Instead, it used means that were unnecessarily broad. The Court asked: "Would we allow the police to search the sacred precincts of marital bedrooms for telltale signs of the use of contraceptives?"[42] Such an idea is "repulsive to the notions of privacy surrounding the marriage relationship."[43] The Court noted:

> We deal with a right of privacy older than the Bill of Rights—older than our political parties, older than our school system. Marriage is a coming together for better or for worse, hopefully enduring, and intimate to the degree of being sacred.[44]

The Connecticut statute was ruled unconstitutional because it would require government to acquire information about an individual's activities within one of the zones of privacy, the marital relationship. Government, despite its enormous investigative powers, must not intrude upon these areas.

Computerized Records

In 1977, in *Whalen* v. *Roe,*[45] the Court considered the constitutionality of a New York statute that required recording in a centralized computer file the names and addresses of all persons who had obtained a doctor's prescription for certain drugs. The drugs included, but were not limited to, those that have an illegal market. A lower court had ruled that creating such a computer file invaded a constitutionally protected zone of privacy, the doctor-patient relationship, and that the act invaded this relationship with "a needlessly broad sweep."[46] The lower court also felt that New York State had been unable to demonstrate the necessity for such a computer file system.

Appellants argued that the existence of the file created a genuine concern that the information could become publicly known and would adversely affect their reputations. The possible disclosure would make some patients reluctant to use and some doctors reluctant to prescribe drugs that were medically indicated. The Court, however, did not feel that the program posed a sufficiently grievous threat to the reputation or independence of patients. The Court reasoned that there were three ways in which the public disclosure could occur. First, health department employees might violate the statute by failing, either deliberately or negligently, to maintain proper security. Second, a patient or doctor might be accused of a violation and the file might be offered as evidence in a judicial proceeding. Third, a doctor, pharmacist, or patient might reveal information on a prescription form. The Court considered each in turn. First, there is nothing in the experience of other states that have had similar programs to indicate that the security provisions of the program would be administered improperly. The Court also did not see the remote possibility of the occurrence of the second instance as a sufficient reason for invalidating the entire patient identification program. Many states recognize the physician-patient privilege, which precludes some records being admitted into evidence. The Court considered the third instance as being unrelated to the computerization of the file.

Concerning the issue of patients and doctors being reluctant to use or prescribe drugs, the Court responded that there are a "host of other unpleasant invasions of privacy that are associated with many facets of health care."[47] The Court observed that it is an essential part of medical practices today that patients disclose private medical information to doctors, hospital personnel, insurance companies, and public health agencies, even when such disclosures may reflect unfavorably on their character. While the record indicates that some use of drugs had been discouraged because information about who is using them is readily available in a computer file, the record also indicates that 100,000 prescriptions continue to be filled each month.

The Court also pointed out that no individual has been deprived of the right to decide independently, with the advice of his or her doctor, to acquire or to use needed medication. New York State has not totally prohibited the use of particular drugs nor does the state require the consent of any official or third party to prescribe the drugs. The decision to use or prescribe is left entirely to the physician and the patient.

The Court also considered the significant state interest involved. New York State has a strong interest in preventing drugs being diverted into unlawful channels. To answer the lower court's contention that New York State is unable to demonstrate the necessity for such a computer file system, the Court replied that:

> State legislation which has some effect on individual liberty or privacy may not be held unconstitutional simply because a court finds it unnecessary, in whole or in part. For we have frequently recognized that individual States have broad latitude in experimenting with possible solutions to problems of vital local concern.[48]

For these reasons the Court ruled that the New York statute does not invade the constitutional right to privacy.

Presidential Records

In the 1977 case of *Nixon* v. *Administrator of General Services*[49] the Court considered the constitutionality of the Presidential Recordings and Materials Preservation Act as it related to the 42 million pages of documents and 880 tape recordings of former President Richard M. Nixon. After resigning from the office of president of the United States, Nixon executed a depository agreement with the Administrator of the General Services Administration (GSA). The agreement called for the records and recordings to be stored near Nixon's California home. Neither the former president nor the GSA could gain access to the material without the other's consent. The agreement also called for the eventual destruction of the tapes. After a five-year period GSA would destroy all of the tapes that the former president directed, and after ten years all of the tapes would be destroyed.

After the terms of the agreement were made public, a bill was introduced in Congress that directed GSA to take custody of Nixon's presidential materials and have them screened by government archivists to determine which were private in nature and which had historical value. Three months later the act was passed and then signed into law by President Gerald Ford. Nixon immediately started a court action challenging the constitutionality of the act in part on the grounds that it violated his privacy interests in avoiding disclosure of personal matters.

The Court acknowledged that public officials, including the president, have constitutionally protected privacy rights in that part of their personal life that is unrelated to any acts done by them in their public capacity. The former president had a reasonable expectation of privacy in withholding matters concerning his family or personal finances. The merits of Nixon's claim of invasion of his privacy must be weighed, however, against the public interest in subjecting the presidential materials to archival screening. In this instance, the Court found the former president's interest weaker than that of the appellants in *Whalen*.

For one, the intrusion in this case is very limited. The act mandates promulgation of regulations aimed at preventing undue dissemination of the private materials. The purely private papers would be returned to the former president. The overwhelming bulk of the material relates to the official conduct of the presidency. Some documents and tapes had already been disclosed to the public. In short, the privacy claim related to only a very small fraction of the massive volume of official materials. The Court concluded that the act is the least intrusive manner in which to provide an adequate level of promotion of government interests of overriding importance.

Records Kept by Government

Whalen and *Nixon* indicate some important points about the relationship between government records and the constitutional right to privacy. First, the government's right to reveal information about an individual conflicts with the individual's constitutional right to privacy when the government's action restricts the individual's freedom in the zone of privacy.[50] As we have seen, the Court has so far explicitly enumerated zones of privacy as in activities relating to marriage, procreation, contraception, family relationships, and child rearing and education.[51] The right of association has also been explicitedly placed within this zone of privacy.[52] In 1992 the Court said that "[t]hese matters, involving the most intimate and personal choices a person may make in a lifetime, choices central to personal dignity and autonomy"[53] are central to liberty because they "define one's own concept of existence, of meaning, of the universe, and of the mystery of human life."[54] Beliefs about these matters would not define personhood if they were formed under the compulsion of government.[55]

Second, persons do not lose their constitutional right to privacy because the records are being kept or held by a government agency. The protection of zones of privacy must include the right to prevent the disclosure of information held by government. This is so even if the information is collected pursuant to a valid governmental objective.[56]

Third, the right to privacy is not absolute. Exceptions are made for information that violates the zones of privacy when the government's interest in disclosure outweighs the individual's privacy interests. In *Whalen* it was noted that a statute that resulted in a serious deprivation of privacy would still be consistent with the Constitution if it promoted a compelling state interest.[57] The courts thus apply a balancing approach to questions of disclosural privacy, weighing each competing interest against the other.

Library Records

Libraries are used by people to make the kind of personal and intimate decisions that fall within the constitutional zones of privacy. It is also clear that library patrons take it for granted that these records will not be available for public scrutiny. Otherwise they might avoid exploring certain information and ideas and making their own decisions about their value. If library patrons have a privacy interest in these records, the courts will weigh this interest against the public's interest in knowing about these records.

In 1989 the Court considered whether disclosing the contents of FBI criminal identification files, known as rap sheets, to a third party constituted an unwarranted invasion of personal privacy. The U.S. Freedom of Information Act (FOIA), which governs disclosure of information collected or compiled by the federal government, makes provisions for safeguarding the personal privacy of individuals in accordance with the Constitution. Under Exemption 7(C)[58] of that law, records that "could reasonably be expected to constitute an unwarranted invasion of personal privacy" are exempt from disclosure. The Court stated that whether disclosure of a private document is warranted under this exemption turns on the nature of the requested document and its relationship to the basic purpose of FOIA.[59] It does not depend on the particular purpose for which the document is being requested nor does it depend on who is requesting it.

The Court determined that the purpose of FOIA was the right of citizens to be informed about what their government is up to. "Official information that sheds light on an agency's performance of its statutory duties falls squarely within that statutory purpose."[60] The Court concluded: "That purpose, however, is not fostered by disclosure of information about private citizens that is accumulated in various governmental files but that reveals little or nothing about an agency's own conduct." In these cases, the requester is not trying to discover anything about the conduct of the agency that has possession of the records. "Indeed, response to this request would not shed any light on the conduct of any Government agency or official."[61] In this case the Court that found the public's interest in rap sheets falls outside that which FOIA was enacted to serve.[62]

Do library records about individual patrons fall outside FOIA's public interest? Do the records kept on individuals reveal anything about what government is up to? These questions have not been directly addressed by the Court. The relationship between such records and both federal and state FOIAs, is dealt with in the next chapter.

ENDNOTES

1. *Roe* v. *Wade*, 410 U.S. 113 at 152 (1973).
2. Dissenting opinion of Justice Black in *Griswold* v. *Connecticut*, 381 U.S. 479 at 509 (1965).
3. Dissenting opinion in *Olmstead* at 478 (1928).
4. Majority opinion in *Katz* v. *United States*, 389 U.S. 347 at 350–351 (1967).
5. Industrial Foundation of the South v. Texas Industrial Accident Board, 540 S.W.2d 668 at 679 (1976), certiorari denied 430 U.S. 931.
6. *Whalen* v. *Roe*, 429 U.S. 589 at 599–600 (1975).
7. *Industrial Foundation of the South* at 679.
8. As stated by Justice Brandeis in *Olmstead*, at 478:
   The makers of our Constitution undertook to secure conditions favorable to the pursuit of happiness. They recognized the significance of man's spiritual nature, of his feelings, and of his intellect. They knew that only a part of the pain, pleasure and satisfactions of life are to be found in material things. They sought to protect Americans in their beliefs, their thoughts, their emotions and their sensations. They conferred as against the Government, the right to be let alone—the most comprehensive of rights and the right most valued by civilized men. To protect that right, every unjustifiable intrusion by the Government upon the privacy of the individual, whatever the means employed, must be deemed a violation. . . .
9. *Stanley* v. *Georgia*, 394 U.S. 557 at 564 (1969).
10. *Griswold* at 491.
11. *Griswold* at 486.
12. In his dissenting opinion to *Griswold* at 508, Justice Black said:
    The Court talks about a constitutional 'right of privacy' as though there is some constitutional provision or provisions forbidding any law ever to be passed which might abridge the 'privacy' of individuals. But there is not. There are, of course, guarantees in certain specific constitutional provisions which are designed in part to protect privacy at certain times and places with respect to certain activities.
13. Justice Douglas's dissent in *Poe* v. *Ullman*, 367 U.S. 497 at 521 (1961).
14. *Pierce* v. *Society of Sisters*, 268 U.S. 33 (1925).

15. *Meyer* v. *Nebraska*, 262 U.S. 390 (1923).
16. *Martin* v. *Struthers*, 319 U.S. 141 at 143 (1943).
17. *Wieman* v. *Updegraff*, 344 U.S. 183 at 195 (1952).
18. *NAACP* v. *Alabama*, 357 U.S. 449 at 460 (1958).
19. Ibid. at 463.
20. *NAACP* v. *Button*, 371 U.S. 415 at 430–431 (1963).
21. *Schware* v. *Board of Bar Examiners*, 353 U.S. 233 at 244 (1957).
22. *Griswold* at 483.
23. *Griswold* at 483.
24. The Third Amendment in part states that:
    No soldier shall, in time of peace be quartered in any house, without the consent of the Owner, nor in time of war, but in a manner to be prescribed by law.
25. The Fourth Amendment states that:
    The right of the people to be secure in their persons, houses, papers, and effects, against unreasonable searches and seizures, shall not be violated, and no warrants shall issue, but upon probable cause, supported by oath or affirmation, and particularly describing the place to be searched, and the persons or things to be seized.
26. *Entick* v. *Carrington*, 19 Howell's State Trials, col. 1029.
27. *Frank* v. *Maryland*, 359 U.S. 360 at 363 (1959).
28. *Mapp* v. *Ohio*, 367 U.S. 643 at 656 (1961).
29. *Griswold* at 484.
30. *Katz* v. *United States*, 389 U.S. 347 at 351 (1967).
31. The Fifth Amendment states:
    "No person shall be held to answer for a capital, or otherwise infamous crime, unless on a presentment or indictment of a Grand Jury, except in cases arising in the land or naval forces, or in the militia, when in actual service in time or war or public danger; nor shall any person be subject for the same offense to be twice put in jeopardy of life or limb; nor shall be compelled in any criminal case to be a witness against himself, nor be deprived or life, liberty, or property, without due process of law; nor shall private property be taken for public use without just compensation." The Self–Incrimination Clause states: ". . . nor shall be compelled in any criminal case to be a witness against himself. . . ."
32. *Griswold* at 484.
33. *Boyd* v. *United States*, 116 U.S. 616 at 630 (1886).
34. *Tehan* v. *U.S.*, 382 U.S. 406 at 416 (1966).
35. *Griswold* at 488–489.
36. *Griswold* at 491.
37. The first clause of the Fourteenth Amendment states:
    1. All persons born or naturalized in the United States, and subject to the jurisdiction thereof, are citizens of the United States and of the State wherein they reside. No State shall make or enforce any law which shall abridge the privileges, or immunities of citizens of the United States; nor shall any state deprive any per-

son of life, liberty, or property, without due process of law; nor
deny to any person within its jurisdiction the equal protection of
the laws.

38. *Meyer* at 399 (1923).
39. *Palko* v. *Connecticut*, 302 U.S. 319 at 325 (1937). Rights that are "fundamental" or "implicit in the concept of ordered liberty" are explicated.
40. *Katz* at 350 fn.5.
41. 381 U.S. 479 (1965).
42. Ibid. at 485.
43. Ibid. at 485–486.
44. Ibid. at 486.
45. 429 U.S. 589.
46. Ibid. at 596.
47. Ibid. at 602.
48. Ibid. at 597.
49. 433 U.S. 425.
50. *Industrial Foundation of the South* at 680–681.
51. *Roe* at 152–153.
52. *Griswold* at 484.
53. *Planned Parenthood of Southeastern Pennsylvania* v. *Casey*, No. 91–744, Slip op. U.S. Supreme Court (June 29, 1992).

    Our law affords constitutional protection to personal decisions
    relating to marriage, procreation, contraception, family relationships, child rearing, and education. *Carey* v. *Population Services International*, 431 U.S., at 685. Our cases recognize the right of
    the individual, married or single, to be free from unwarranted
    governmental intrusion into matters so fundamentally affecting
    a person as the decision whether to bear or beget a child.
    Eisenstadt v. *Baird*. . . . Our precedents have respected the private realm of family life which the state cannot enter. *Prince* v.
    Massachusetts, 321 U.S. 158, 166 (1944). These matters, involving the most intimate and personal choices a person may make in
    a lifetime, choices central to personal dignity and autonomy, are
    central to the liberty protected by the Fourteenth Amendment.
    At the heart of liberty is the right to define one's own concept of
    existence, of meaning, of the universe, and of the mystery of human life. Beliefs about these matters could not define the attributes of personhood were they formed under compulsion of the
    State.

54. Ibid.
55. Ibid.
56. In *Industrial Foundation of the South* at 679 the Supreme Court of
    Texas stated:

    The individual does not forfeit all rights to control access to intimate facts concerning his personal life merely because the State
    has a legitimate interest in obtaining that information.

57. In *Whalen* at 606–607 (1977), Justice Brennan in a concurring opinion said:

> A statute that did effect such a [serious] deprivation [of privacy] would only be consistent with the Constitution if it were necessary to promote a compelling state interest.

58. Section 552(b)(7)(C). See Appendix B.
59. *United States Department of Justice* v. *Reporters Committee for Freedom of the Press*, 489 U.S. 749 at 753 (1989).
60. Ibid. at 773.
61. Ibid.
62. Ibid. at 775.

Part II
Statutory and Other Rights

6
Freedom of Information (Sunshine) Laws

- *What is the relationship between FOIA and the constitutional right to privacy?*
- *What effect do freedom of information laws have on libraries?*
- *How many states afford some form of privacy protection to library patrons' records?*

Libraries encourage their communities to use the facilities, materials, and services that they provide for obtaining ideas and information. In addition, libraries provide educational and recreational programs and materials to enhance the quality of life of the citizens of the community. Libraries encourage patrons to use materials within the library's walls as well as borrow materials for use at home, in the classroom, or at work. Many libraries also make meeting and exhibit spaces available for use by groups and individuals.

Although libraries encourage use, there must be rules for patrons—whether for the use of the facility itself, for use of the library's resources, or some combination of both. These rules must be fair, they must apply to all users, and they must be applied evenly. In order to develop rules for the use of a library, it is necessary to know what a patron's rights may be, how these rights have come about, and what limitations there may be on these rights.

There are a number of instruments that provide library users with rights. In addition to the U.S. Constitution, which has already been discussed, the copyright law, federal and state documents depository laws, freedom of information statutes, state privacy laws, the Americans with Disabilities Act, and state and local statutes establishing publicly-funded libraries form part of the basis for patron use of libraries. In addition, the American Library Association's Library Bill of Rights, Freedom to Read Statement, and related documents on the rights of children in libraries, labeling of library materials, and other issues have been adopted as policy by a large number of libraries. Further, library policies established by library governing bodies extend both rights and responsibilities to patrons.

There is another type of law that creates a right to information for the citizens of the United States. These are the laws at both the federal and state level known as "sunshine" laws or "freedom of information" laws. These laws have had three major effects on libraries. One effect is that libraries can obtain and make available to their patrons the minutes and other records of public boards, commissions, and agencies. A second effect for publicly-funded libraries is that the activities of library governing bodies themselves are subject to state freedom of information laws. The third effect has been the exemption of library circulation records from the freedom of information laws, in almost all states, making a patron's reading habits confidential.

The earliest predecessor to "sunshine" or "freedom of information" laws was the 1789 "housekeeping" statute, which gave federal agencies the authority to regulate their own business, set up filing systems, and keep records. This law gave executive agencies the authority to withhold information and control public availability of records as the agency saw fit. In 1958, Congress reduced the authority of federal agencies to control access to their own records. Then, after eight years of extensive investigative and legislative hearings, Congress eliminated the discretionary authority to withhold information and control the availability of records to the public.

A federal law declaring that the business of government should be conducted openly and that the documents generated by governmental bodies should be available to the public was finally passed by Congress and went into effect on July 4, 1967. That law is the U.S. Freedom of Information Act (FOIA), codified as Title 5 of the United States Code, Section 552. This Act is reprinted in Appendix B. Before the enactment of the Freedom of Information Act, the burden was on the individual to establish a right to examine government records. There were no statutory guidelines or procedures to help a person seeking government records. There was no recourse if access to those records was denied.

The passage of FOIA changed that situation completely. Now, government records in the possession of agencies and departments of the executive branch are accessible to everyone. The burden of proof has shifted from the person seeking the record to the government agency. The need to know requirement has been replaced by the right to know doctrine. Government has to justify the need for secrecy in order to deny access to a record. Under FOIA, federal agencies are required to provide the fullest possible disclosure of information to the public.

The basic purpose behind FOIA is to ensure that an informed citizenry will hold government accountable to the governed and act as a check against corruption. Under this law, an agency may withhold a document only if the information in it falls within one of nine statutory exemptions. These exemptions are:

- matters relating to national defense;
- personnel and medical files;
- records related solely to internal personnel rules and practices of an agency;
- trade secrets or privileged commercial or financial information;
- interagency or intraagency memos or letters;
- certain records or information compiled for law enforcement purposes;
- certain records pertaining to the regulation of financial institutions;
- geological or geophysical information and data, including maps, concerning wells; and
- matters specifically exempted from disclosure by statute.

A decision by an agency to withhold information can be challenged in federal court, with the burden of proof for the withholding falling on the agency.

The policy of the Freedom of Information Act of favoring public access is grounded in the constitutional right to receive and gain access to information and ideas. Its purpose of providing access to government information allows citizens to know what their government is doing. Arbitrarily denying access to important government information abridges the freedoms of speech and of the press as protected by the First Amendment.

The federal Freedom of Information Act includes among its provisions that each agency make available to the public a description of its organization; the method whereby the public may obtain information, records, and decisions and make submittals and requests; rules of procedure; descriptions of forms and how to obtain them; and any fee schedules in effect.

The U.S. Freedom of Information Act concerns only federal agencies and their records, but many states have followed suit and passed legislation modeled on the federal law. The state laws generally cover both state and municipal public agencies. These laws have thrown the business of state and local agencies open to the general public. Since many libraries, whether academic, public, school, or special, are state or local agencies, the meetings of the library governing entities are open to anyone wishing to attend and the records of their activities are also part of the public record.

With freedom of information laws opening up library records in some cases, patron privacy became an issue. Police departments realized that, for example, if a missing suspect in a criminal matter was the parent of a child with a library card, the address of that child acquired from library circulation records could help in locating the suspect. Treasury agents sought circulation records as evidence against patrons they suspected of being "radicals" looking for bomb-building information. Librarians all over the country began to realize that they were being asked to participate in activities that were contrary to the principles that guided them. The American Library Association got many queries from libraries being questioned about patrons by local, state, and federal law enforcement agencies. Many libraries and state library associations sought help from their legislatures to ensure the right to privacy for library patrons.

Over 35 states had some form of protection for library patrons' records in place when the Federal Bureau of Investigation instituted the "Library Awareness Program" in 1985. The program sought to enlist the aid of library staff members in identifying subversives. Since that time, all but five states have passed laws protecting library patron records.

State freedom of information statutes generally have specific exemptions for library circulation records or other records of services used, providing privacy for citizens in regard to the materials that they borrow from public libraries and, in some states, other libraries as well. In some cases, instead of exempting libraries from the state's "sunshine law," a state protects the privacy of library users with statutes passed specifically for that purpose. In addition to the circulation records, a number of states also make reference queries and in-house use of materials confidential.

A state-by-state explanation and description of the laws protecting library user privacy is contained in the authors' earlier volume *Maintaining the Privacy of Library Records : A Handbook and Guide* (Neal-Schuman, 1994).

The American Library Association has developed a policy on the confidentiality of library records that is commonly adopted as part of local library policy. It is particularly helpful in defending patron privacy for the libraries in those five states without specific laws protecting library records.

7
Other Legal Rights

- *What are some of the other statutory rights that library patrons have?*
- *Where can these rights be found?*
- *How does the Americans with Disabilities Act affect the rights of library patrons?*
- *What are some of the rights library patrons have under the copyright laws?*

COPYRIGHT

Library patrons have some extremely important rights under the copyright law of the United States. Sections 107 (Fair Use) and 108 (Reproduction and Distribution by Libraries and Archives) of the current copyright law grant important exceptions for library users to the "exclusive rights" that authors obtain when copyrighting their works.

Specifically, under the fair use exception, for the purpose of criticism, comment, news reporting, teaching, scholarship, or research, a patron may copy portions of a work without infringing the copyright of that work. In determining whether the use made of a work in any particular case is a fair use, the courts look at four factors:

1. The purpose and character of the use, including whether such use is of commercial nature or is for a nonprofit educational purpose.
2. The nature of the copyrighted work, including whether the work is fiction or nonfiction and whether the work is published or unpublished.
3. The amount and substantiality of the portion used in relation to the copyrighted work as a whole.
4. The effect of the use upon the potential market for or value of the copyrighted work.

To protect the rights of all parties—the patron, the author, and the library—unsupervised, coin-operated library copy machines with an appropriate copyright warning should be located conveniently for patron use. The burden of complying with the law's Section 107 fair use clause rests with the library patron.

There is a certain class of library patron that has a broad privilege of fair use under the copyright law: classroom teachers. For scholarly research or for use in teaching or in preparing to teach a class, a teacher may make one copy of: a chapter from a book, an article from a periodical or newspaper, a short story, a short essay or a short poem (whether or not the story, essay, or poem is from a collective work), a chart, a diagram, a drawing, a cartoon, or a picture from a book or periodical or newspaper.

In addition, teachers may also make, or have made, multiple copies (one copy per pupil in a course) for their own classes for discussion or for classroom use. These copies must each include a notice of copyright and the copying must meet the tests of brevity, spontaneity, and cumulative effect as defined in the *Agreement on Guidelines for Classroom Copying in Not-for-Profit Educational Institutions*. The guidelines were agreed upon by a group of publishers, authors, and representatives of educational institutions and were published in the October 14, 1979 *Congressional Record*.

Three recent cases, *Basic Books, Inc., et al.* v. *Kinko's Graphics Corporation*,[1] *American Geophysical Union, et al.* v. *Texaco Inc.*[2], and *Princeton University Press, et al.* v. *Michigan Document Services, Inc. et al.*[3], have caught the attention of librarians across the country because the defendants in all three of these cases asserted a fair use defense and lost.

The defendant in the *Kinko* case, the Kinko's Graphics Corporation, set up copy shops near or on college and university campuses. These copy shops photocopied excerpts from copyrighted books and other materials to create customized anthologies, in accordance with the requirements of professors, for instructional use in college and university classrooms—a practice sometimes called "professor publishing." Kinko's neither sought permission to use these materials nor paid royalties to the copyright holders.

When a group of publishers sued, Kinko's Graphics Corporation asserted fair use as a defense, pointing out that these anthologies were generated for a particular course and bore the course name and the professor's name as well. Kinko's further asserted that the purpose of these anthologies was expressly educational and that the copying came under the guidelines for classroom copying.

In weighing the four fair use factors, the court found for the publishers on all four grounds. The court stated that Kinko's, as a profit-making entity, was not protected under the guidelines for classroom copying. In addition, the court noted that Kinko's had created a new and lucrative nationwide business based on the making of these customized anthologies. Kinko's was ordered to stop the practice and to pay statutory damages of $510,000 for willful infringement.

The *Kinko* case set the precedent for another similar case. Michigan Doument Services (MDS), another for-profit corporation, photocopied and bound together academic materials—which a professor had selected and arranged—into a "coursepack" for sale to students enrolled in the professor's class. Princeton University Press, Macmillan, and St. Martin's Press brought suit against MDS. MDS, like Kinko's, asserted the fair use defense. MDS claimed it should have the same rights and privileges as students, who probably could have individually photocopied the excerpts without infringing copyrights. The court rejected that defense, stating that the defendant was taking the property of another without right or permission, for personal gain. In finding willful infringement, the court ordered that the defendants pay statutory damages of $5,000 per infringed work plus reasonable counsel fees, and enjoined them from copying any of the publishers' works without permission.

Two immediate effects from the *Kinko* and *Michigan Document Services* cases are:

- an increase in requests for permissions; and
- an increase in the number of items on reserve in academic libraries.

The number of copies of photocopied materials that may be put on reserve is of concern to librarians, who may turn to the American Library Association's "Model Policy Concerning College and University Photocopying for Classroom Research and Library Reserve Use" for suggestions on what is permissible. However, it should be noted that these guidelines have been the subject of some criticism because they use the classroom guidelines for photocopying as their basis, a model that does not transfer well to the matter of reserves. For example, classroom guidelines allow one copy per pupil, but the point of putting copies on reserve is to have students share a small number of copies. Since there are no court cases on the issue, the matter of reserves remains an untested area of the law at this time. Meanwhile, librarians must proceed with caution, using their best judgment as to the number of copies of a particular item to put on reserve.

The *Texaco* case deals with the issue of fair use in the corporate context. Texaco, the petroleum giant, employs a number of research scientists. The company keeps a large library of technical journals in each of its locations. These journals or their tables of contents were, in the past, circulated to these researchers, who often ordered copies made or made copies of articles themselves. These copies were put to various uses; some were brought into the research laboratories to keep the original journal from being damaged by laboratory substances and some were put away by scientists for future use. When these practices were discovered, the publishers of several of these journals joined together and sued Texaco for copyright infringement. Texaco asserted the fair use defense. The court found that Texaco scientists were infringing the copyrights of the holders. In its decision, the court found that Texaco did not meet the fair use criteria in using copies as substitutes for the original copyrighted text. Profit-making organizations, in light of the *Texaco* decision, must now pay royalties for each copy made from a journal or must limit employees to use of the circulating copies of the journals themselves.

In addition to the privilege of fair use as codified in Section 107 of the copyright law, Section 108 of the law contains additional privileges for library patrons. This section of the law makes possible the interlibrary loan of copies of journal, periodical, serial, and magazine articles. Certain rules must be observed in regard to such copying. One copy can be made if

- the copying is without direct or indirect commercial advantage;
- the collection of the library is either open to the public or available to outside persons doing research in a specialized field;
- a notice of copyright appears on the copy;
- the copy becomes the property of the requester;
- the copying is isolated and unrelated;
- the copyright notice prescribed under the law is displayed at the place where orders are taken.

This right to obtain articles through interlibrary loan is a distinct advantage for library patrons, even though the privilege is contingent on meeting all the above requirements.

In addition, the CONTU (National Commission on New Technological Uses of Copyrighted Works) rule of five applies to each library performing interlibrary loans. That rule restricts a library to requesting, in one calendar year, no more than five copies of articles (the same one five times or five different ones or any combination) from one title (for example, *Time*) that is less than five years old. It is the borrowing library's responsibility to keep records of such requests. If the borrowing library needs further copies after it reaches the five-requests-from-one-title limit, it is obligated to either purchase a subscription of the periodical or to pay the publisher (usually through the Copyright Clearance Center) a royalty for each copy made.

FEDERAL AND STATE DOCUMENTS DEPOSITORY SYSTEMS

The documents depository law of the United States and individual state laws modeled on it provide a system whereby selected federal and state documents (the publications of federal and state agencies) are made available to the public in all types of libraries. The federal documents depository law stipulates that there be two types of depositories: full depositories (which receive all of the documents that are designated as depository items) and partial depositories (which receive documents only from agencies that are of particular interest to the library and its clientele, although a partial depository is allowed to choose to obtain all depository items). Each full depository supervises several partial depositories. Because there is a steady stream of federal documents (full depositories receive boxes of items at least weekly) space considerations may limit a library to obtaining only those documents of high interest.

The documents are sent to depository libraries without charge, but to become a depository library the library must agree to allow the general public to use the collection and to provide reference service in regard to the materials. Some public libraries have applied for and obtained federal and/or state documents depository status. Academic libraries, both publicly funded and private, are usually partial depositories as well. Law school libraries are invariably part of the depository program. One effect of this access rule is to make it possible for someone who is not a student at a major private university to use its documents collection, since even the most exclusive institution must agree to allow public use in order to receive depository library status.

Many state libraries are both federal and state full documents depositories, supervising the partial depositories in their own state—and in some cases those in contiguous states also. In general, public, academic, and special libraries that are partial federal depository libraries are usually depositories for state documents as well. On the other hand, a number of public libraries prefer to serve only as state documents depositories. There is a much lower number of state documents produced each year than federal documents, proportional to the size of government at the federal and state levels. State documents depository laws are usually modeled closely on the federal documents law. The result is that state documents depositories must agree to provide access to the documents by allowing the public to use them and also must agree to provide reference service for them.

These depository laws insure that the public has free access to the information generated by federal and state agencies. This includes the laws passed by Congress and state legislatures, census data, consumer information, crime statistics, education reports, health research, environmental information, and a host of other topics. Some of these topics are covered by agencies at both state and federal levels. Although many of the documents are available for purchase from the federal or state government, depository laws guarantee that users have free access to government publications.

SPECIAL SERVICES TO THE BLIND AND PHYSICALLY HANDICAPPED

The federal government has produced instructional materials for blind students for well over a century—beginning in 1879 with the opening of a reading room for the blind in Washington, D.C., under the supervision of the Librarian of Congress. In 1913, Congress mandated that a copy of each braille book made under government subsidy must be deposited in the Library of Congress.

Talking books were introduced in 1934 as part of the program called Library Service to the Blind. With this innovation, blind persons who were not students became eligible to receive braille or recorded materials, which included a full range of titles for children, young adults, and adults. Those with physical handicaps and learning disabilities eventually also became eligible to use the service.

Today the law (Title 20, Section 351a of the United States Code) defines "library services for the physically handicapped" as

> the providing of library services, through public or other nonprofit libraries, agencies, or organizations, to physically handicapped persons (including the blind and other visually handicapped) certified by competent authority as unable to read or to use conventional printed materials as a result of phyical limitations.

All 50 states plus the District of Columbia, Puerto Rico, and the Virgin Islands participate in this program, which provides recorded books, the necessary players, and specialized service tailored to the individual's needs and interests. These materials are provided without cost to the patron and are sent through the mail as free matter for the blind. Any public or state library can supply information about the program and can certify users as eligible for the service.

AMERICANS WITH DISABILITIES ACT (ADA)

The Americans with Disabilities Act of 1990 (ADA) assures that citizens with disabilities may participate in public services. The act has five titles: Title I covers employment, Title II covers public services, Title III covers public accommodations and services operated by private entities, Title IV covers telecommunications, and Title V contains miscellaneous provisions.

Title II, Public Services, applies to publicly-funded libraries. This title covers anyone defined as "an individual with a disability who, with or without reasonable modification to rules, policies, or practices, the removal of architectural, communications, or transportation barriers, or the provision of auxiliary aids and services, meets the essential eligibility for the receipt of services or the participation in programs or activities provided by a public entity." Qualified individuals with disabilities are protected from discrimination on the basis of disability in the services, programs, or activities of state and local governments. Title II also extends the earlier prohibition against discrimination in federally-assisted programs established by section 504 of the Rehabilitation Act of 1973 to all activities of state and local governments, whether these activities receive federal financial assistance or not.

ADA requirements that apply to state and local agencies and institutions (with some exceptions for agencies or institutions employing fewer than 50 people) include:

- Designation of an employee to coordinate ADA compliance.
- Adoption and publication of grievance procedures.
- Review of policies and practices to assure nondiscrimination.
- Any brochures or other information about agency services must inform individuals with disabilities about services available to them. This information must be made available in a method of communication that can be used by an individual with disabilities, with auxiliary aids and services provided as needed.

- Existing facilities must conduct a "program access" self-evaluation to assess whether or not facilities and services are accessible. During the self-evaluation process, interested persons and individuals with disabilities must be consulted.
- Major alterations and new construction begun after January 26, 1992, must meet the requirements of either the Uniform Federal Accessibility Standards or the ADA Accessibility Guidelines.

Libraries that lack easy access for persons with disabilities may qualify to apply for Library Services and Construction Act (LSCA) funds to provide such access.

STATE LAWS

State and local laws, too numerous and varied to be reviewed here, also provide privileges for library patrons. State laws enable municipal establishment of public libraries. Sometimes such laws designate a general scheme of governance. State libraries, with a varying scope of responsibility, are also the product of state law. Library cooperatives, usually comprising a network of all types of libraries, are also the result of enabling state legislation. In some states, the law allows citizen use of publicly-funded academic libraries. State law determines who has the responsibility for school libraries. In some places, law libraries that are part of the judicial system are open to the public under state law. Under the rubric of state law, state documents depository systems provide public access to state government publications. State freedom of information laws provide citizen access to the business of state and local public bodies. As we have seen, confidentiality of library records laws are in place in most states. These, and other state laws regarding libraries, provide a host of services and rights for the library patron.

LOCAL LAWS

Local charters or ordinances may dictate what services a local library is expected to provide. Charters or ordinances may mandate the type of library governance that will be in place. Local budgets, passed by municipal governing authorities, determine staffing levels and materials and equipment purchases.

ENDNOTES

1. 758 F. Supp. 1522 (S.D.N.Y. 1992).
2. 802 F.Supp. 1 (S.D.N.Y. 1992).
3. Case No. 92-CV-71029-DT (E.D. Mich. So. Div. June 9, 1994).

8
Other Rights

* *Do ALA library policies affect the rights of library patrons?*
* *Are library patron rights affected by librarians' codes of ethics?*
* *What are some basic rights that all library patrons have?*

LIBRARY POLICIES

Library policies also affect the rights of library patrons. Most libraries have adopted the American Library Association's (ALA) Library Bill of Rights as part of their policy statements. The Bill of Rights itself contains six clauses that place upon libraries the responsibility to:

* provide resources without regard to the origin, background or beliefs of the authors;
* provide a wide range of materials on all sides of an issue;
* challenge efforts at censorship;
* cooperate with persons and groups concerned with resisting abridgement of free expression and access to ideas;
* allow the use of all library materials by all patrons, regardless of origin, age, background, or views; and
* be fair in allowing exhibit and meeting space use.

These clauses are all-important in protecting the rights of patrons.

The broad themes of the Library Bill of Rights have been interpreted in a number of additional policy statements known as Interpretations of the Library Bill of Rights. These include statements on the subjects of:

* challenged materials;
* diversity in collection development;

- free access to libraries for minors;
- access for children and young people to videotapes and other nonprint formats;
- access to resources and services in the school library media program;
- access without regard to gender or sexual orientation;
- economic barriers to information access;
- expurgation of library materials;
- restricting access to library materials;
- evaluating library collections, exhibit space, and bulletin boards;
- library-initiated programs as a resource;
- meeting rooms;
- labeling of materials; and
- the right to free expression.

Libraries that adopt these interpretations as policy offer important protections for library patrons.

CODES OF ETHICS

The American Library Association (ALA) and other library associations have developed codes of ethics for members of the profession. The ALA statement has clauses that require librarians to provide equity in their service to patrons and to provide patrons with confidentiality in regard to their queries. Librarians who subscribe to these codes uphold a high level of respect for their users.

BASIC RIGHTS

Library users have been given a number of specific rights in regard to library services. However, it is important to remember that library users have constitutional rights as well. Freedom of speech, the right to assemble, freedom from discrimination, the right to due process, and the right to privacy exist simultaneously and continuously.

SUMMARY

It may be surprising to some librarians to learn how much legislation there is to buttress the rights of library users. This information has not generally been gathered in one place for perusal.

The importance of library service is manifested in the strong support it has in our legal structure. From the broadest levels of the law—the U.S. Constitution—to those whose jurisdiction is local—municipal ordinances—there is law that affects libraries and their patrons.

Librarians have always accepted, indeed welcomed, their responsibility to help their constituencies obtain the informational, educational, and recreational materials that they require. Some types of libraries, especially public libraries, have not always received the kind of financial support that makes it possible to do the job as fully as the laws require. If, as the Third Circuit U.S. Court of Appeals said, public libraries are "the quintessential locus of the receipt of information,"[1] it would seem that they should be at the top of priorities when local and county budgets are developed.

If school libraries have "special characteristics" that are "especially important for the recognition of the First Amendment rights of students,"[2] then clearly these libraries should occupy a position of importance in the school system hierarchy that is not apparent today.

Those in positions of governance must be made aware that there is a strong recognition in the law and in the policies of libraries that these institutions serve an essential role in our democratic society. Such recognition could result in the kind of support that is needed to bring these information agencies into the next century equipped to do the job that no one else can do—provide every citizen with the informational and recreational resources needed to function effectively and to enhance the quality of life.

ENDNOTES

1. *Kreimer* v. *Bureau of Police for Town of Morristown*, 958 F.2d 1242 at 1255 (1992).
2. *Board of Education* v. *Pico*, 457 U.S. 853 at 869 (1982).

Part III
Library Applications

9

Legal Constraints on the Library User

- *What rules can libraries make to assure that the rights of one library patron do not impinge on the rights of other patrons?*
- *Can a library legally ban a patron from using the library?*
- *What are the most important factors to consider in making library rules and regulations?*
- *What steps should be taken in developing library rules that affect patrons?*

A number of laws support library patrons' rights to library service. With rights come responsibilities. What responsibilities do patrons have in exerting their library rights? What rules can libraries make to ensure that the rights of one library patron do not impinge on the rights of other patrons? This chapter considers these questions.

As long as they have been in existence, libraries have had rules for use of materials, programs, equipment, and facilities. But for a short time beginning in 1991, while the *Kreimer* case (also discussed in Chapter 3 under "Libraries and the Right to Information") was pending and after it was first decided, there were questions raised about the ability of public library governing bodies to make such rules. The case involved Richard Kreimer, a homeless man who frequented the Morristown, New Jersey, public library, who brought suit against the library for rules generated by the its board of trustees. Under these rules, Kreimer was expelled from the library for several reasons, among them his strong odor. Kreimer alleged that the rules were specifically aimed at him and that, on their face, they violated his rights.

When the lower court sided with Kreimer, libraries across the country worried that chaos would prevail if trustees of public libraries were denied the right to make rules for library use. However, in an appeal of the case from the District Court, the Third Circuit Court of Appeals found that the library was a limited public forum and that rules necessary to ensure an orderly use of the institution for the purposes for which it existed could be put in place. The court of appeals further found that persons using the library for other than its recognized purposes could be expelled. Even though the case is limited in its jurisdiction, it has been widely quoted and depended on as a guide for public libraries all over the country. This is especially true because there are no other cases dealing with these particular issues.

The *Kreimer* case underscored some advice that an attorney consulted about the imposition of rules by a public agency might emphasize. That advice would be to generate reasonable rules and to apply them evenhandedly and consistently. For example, assume that a library has just instituted a policy that all patrons must put down a deposit of $10, unless exempted because of hardship, to take out a *Chilton's Auto Repair Manual.* The policy has come into being because the cost of replacing lost and unreturned manuals has become prohibitive. Indeed, such volumes are no longer in print and cannot, therefore, be replaced at a reasonable cost. The policy is meant to emphasize the seriousness of the commitment of the borrower and to be an incentive for people to return the materials. Such a policy must be applied to all patrons. If there are to be exceptions, for hardship perhaps, those exceptions should be clearly spelled out and made publicly available.

Selective application of rules leads to trouble. If circulation staff makes ad hoc exceptions to the deposit requirement for patrons they know well, patrons who are required to follow the rule may overhear and protest the policy as unfair and discriminatory. It may be true that the patron excused from the deposit requirement is always prompt in returning materials. However, the rule states that all patrons borrowing the particular items must make the deposit, except for the hardship exception (for which specific proof is required). The staff *must* enforce the rule as it is stated.

The fact that rules for use of the library must be enforced and that enforcement must be evenhanded has important implications for library-governing authorities. Policymakers should not institute a rule that is not truly enforceable, that violates an American Library Association recommended policy, or that by its nature cries out for selective enforcement.

An example of an unenforceable rule might be one that says that children under the age of ten can use the library for only two hours on any day. If the library has adopted the Library Bill of Rights, the first question that should be addressed is whether such a rule would violate it or its interpretations. If it should survive that test (it would not) or if the library governing body has not adopted the Library Bill of Rights, then the question becomes, "Is the rule truly enforceable or must there be so many exceptions that it isn't a rule at all?" Further questions immediately arise. How is the age of a child to be determined? What if a child is almost through with the research for a paper due the next day? Another 15 minutes to a half hour and the job would be done. The application of a little imagination can lead to a long list of other reasons the two-hour rule makes no sense. How is it to be enforced? What if a child is accompanied by a parent who has work to do for a college course and that work is not finished when the child's two-hour limit has passed? Is the child to be expelled from the library to wait in the car for the parent? What happens when there is disagreement about when a youngster came into the library? Will children's hands be stamped with a color denoting the hour of arrival? Is a child who entered the library at 2:12 p.m. to be ushered out at 4:12 p.m.? Who on the staff has the time to enforce the rule? While each library is different and must determine for itself what rules to make and implement, care must be taken at all times to avoid instituting rules and policies that inhibit the patrons' basic right to full library service.

GENERAL RULES OF CONDUCT

A substantial number of policies affect all patrons. Some of these are broad in their coverage, e.g., collection development policies. Other policies deal with only one segment of the library population, like children, or one portion of the library's services, like meeting rooms. Libraries do have the ability to make rules in order to provide equitable, convenient, productive, and pleasant library service for all patrons.

Many libraries have general rules of conduct for patrons using the library. The American Library Association's Intellectual Freedom Committee has developed two general sets of guidelines for developing such rules ("Guidelines on Patron Behavior and Library Use" and "Guidelines for the Development and Implementation of Policies and Procedures Protecting Access to Library Reserves, Services, and Facilities"), and some state library associations have developed model rules. Such rules of conduct generally include:

1. The library is for all to use and that it is expected that one patron will not impinge the rights of other patrons;
2. The use of tables and seating areas is limited to study and use of library materials;
3. Patrons are to use a pay phone for making their calls;
4. Only quiet conversations that do not disturb others are permitted;
5. There is to be no eating or drinking in the library except at library-approved events, or, in some libraries, in designated places;
6. There is to be no smoking in the library building;
7. The only animals permitted in the library are those needed to assist persons with disabilities;
8. There is to be no sleeping in the library;
9. There is to be no soliciting or proselytizing;
10. Patrons must wear shoes, shirts, and attire appropriate to a public setting;
11. Verbal or physical abuse toward any individual is prohibited;
12. Drunkenness, disorderly behavior, or other improper acts that are subject to prosecution under criminal or civil codes of the law are prohibited;
13. The use of abusive, insulting, or threatening language to any person in or on library property will be cause for removal;
14. Bathrooms are not to be used for bathing or as changing rooms; and
15. The failure to adhere to these rules may result in the loss of the offender's library privileges.

In addition, there may be statements in the rules about littering, the defacing of library property, appropriate use of elevators, and other situations specific to a given library.

When putting rules of conduct in place, it is important for library governing authorities and staffs to tailor the rules to the library's particular situation. And it is very important to remember that the staff members who are on duty at a particular time must enforce the rules that are in place fairly and evenhandedly.

SPECIFIC POLICIES AND RULES FOR SPECIFIC SITUATIONS

Does the library staff know what to do if someone suddenly appears to be ill? Does it know what to do if someone snatches a patron's purse and flees the building? What if a patron persists in following a page as she shelves materials? Are unattended young children being left for long periods of time in the children's department? Are there patrons who stay for hours at the public access computers? Do teenagers gather in large groups in the periodicals department, making adult patrons reluctant to use the area? Has a patron taken to making suggestive remarks to the reference staff? Is there a local group of parents objecting to several titles in the school or public library? Is there a priority order for requests for use of the meeting rooms? Does staff know that the circulation records are confidential? What materials are allowed in the exhibit cases? Has vandalism occurred in the rest rooms?

These and myriad other questions have led to policies being put into place. Because it is better to anticipate before something happens than to react afterward, libraries adopt a number of standard policies affecting patrons, revise old policies, and adopt new policies as needed in order to deal with an ever-changing world. These policies usually include the following topics:

- Rules of behavior
- Dealing with emergencies
- Intellectual freedom
- Selection of materials
- Confidentiality of library records
- Weeding and disposal of library materials
- Acceptance of gifts
- Circulation of materials
- Unattended children
- Technology for public use
- Sexual harassment
- Public use of library equipment
- Exhibits
- Meeting room use
- Cooperative arrangements
- Fees for services
- Complaint procedures
- Training and continuing education of staff

Different types of libraries have different policy requirements for dealing with their users. Libraries in commercial establishments such as insurance companies and law firms probably have no need for a policy on unattended children. Academic libraries may need a policy on use of rare books. School libraries may need a special policy dealing with the reproduction or editing of audiovisual materials and applicable copyright restrictions. Public libraries may need policies on dealing with graffiti both inside and outside of the building.

Libraries have the right to make policies and to write rules and regulations in order to make the use of the library a positive experience for everyone. For any subject that needs to be addressed, a fair policy that protects user rights and that is administered in an evenhanded way is one that should be able to withstand any challenge.

POLICY DEVELOPMENT AND REVIEW

A review of some general policies, their implication for patrons, and their application can be helpful for those who must oversee the operation of libraries. A suggested structured process for the generation of policies and rules to deal with specific types of problem patrons can serve as a model for those who may be faced with similar situations in the future.

While there are similarities between and among all types of libraries, there are always some differences, whether the libraries in question are of like types or not. The differences mandate that each library generate policies tailored to its own situation.

Remember that library policies and rules are put in place with the purpose of maintaining a safe environment for both library users and staff. The policies and rules must comply with federal, state, and local laws while providing equal access for the library's community to its resources.

The authors have created the following process for developing and maintaining effective policies and procedures.

1. *Select a committee*
Someone must assume responsibility for the policy review and development process. This is generally a committee responsibility, and the composition of the committee is based on the type of library involved. Representation from the governing entity, the administration of the library, and the staff may be appropriate. On the other hand, a staff and administration committee may complete the process and recommend changes to existing policies, or entirely new ones, to the governing authorities. Each library must decide the committee membership for its particular situation.

2. *Review documents already in place*
It is important when developing policies to review the mission statement of the library. In addition, the institution's goals and objectives must be scrutinized. Finally, existing policies must be checked for effectiveness, fairness, currency, and legality.

3. *Acquire sample policies*

If there are any policies that seem to need revision or if there is a need for a new policy, then the next step is to acquire samples. These samples should be used as idea generators and studied and analyzed for obvious advantages and disadvantages.

4. *Search the literature, including state and local laws and ALA policies and guidelines*

The library literature contains much valuable information on policies, including tips on the basic subjects as well as the current "hot" topics. New problems emerge as a result of the changes in technology as well as in society at large.

It is important to remember that there are a number of laws that libraries can rely on in dealing with problems. These include laws on theft of library materials, disorderly conduct, drug use and possession, public indecency, assault and battery, intoxication, harassment, and other statutes. The library's research should include an overview of the relevant laws. Citation may be made to the relevant statutes in policy statements. Library staffs should be made aware of these laws and of the library's procedure for employing them when needed. Training sessions are important to ensure any actions taken are appropriate.

5. *Talk to people*

Discuss the issues for consideration for policy development with the library staff, members of the library community if appropriate, and librarians who already have similar policies in place.

6. *Draft a statement that demonstrates what the revised or new policy is to accomplish and test it*

This process of putting into basic language what the new or revised policy is meant to do will help to develop a final policy that will work. Specify the policy's objective by explaining in simple terms exactly what it is to accomplish. Have this explanation read by people who are outside the process to see if its meaning is clear.

7. *Draft the new or revised policy*

Write the policy, using all of the information gathered plus the concepts stated in step 6. Sometimes all that is necessary is to modify one of the policies gathered from other libraries; in other cases, no model may work in the given situation.

8. *Ask others to look at the new or revised policy*

Send the new or revised policy to administration, staff, legal counsel, and governing authorities for a first review. Ask for identification of potential problems and of possible impacts.

9. *Revise draft of new or revised policy*
Based on the comments received, adjust the draft policy appropriately. Any revised or new policy should be reviewed, as a final step before recommending implementation, for adherence to the library's mission, goals, and objectives, and for compliance with applicable laws.

10. *Recommend adoption of new or revised policy by governing authority*
The process that led to the new or revised policy in its final form should be reviewed for the governing authorities. A summary of the steps and the decision-making process is usually helpful to them.

11. *Communicate*
Staff should be kept fully informed about the progress of a new or revised policy. Communication is important in ensuring that a policy is accepted by the people who are responsible for its implementation, whether or not they were directly involved in its development.

12. *Design procedures*
After the adoption of a policy, procedures must be designed to implement it. This can be done at the time of the policy writing or later. Staff input is essential during this step, since they know what works and what doesn't. Legality can be an issue with procedures, as well as with the policies they are meant to implement, so review by legal counsel is recommended.

13. *Publicize*
Make the policies and procedures known to both staff and users. Posting them on user and staff bulletin boards, as well as creating brochures, writing articles for newsletters and newspapers can all be effective communication methods.

14. *Designate someone to monitor effectiveness*
Once a new or revised policy is in effect, it is necessary to designate a staff member or the library director to monitor the policy's effectiveness until the regular review process kicks in.

15. *Carry out regular review*
All policies are subject to regular review, to ascertain whether

or not they accomplish the expected purpose. This review can take place annually or at some other appropriate interval.

SUMMARY

Policies must be written down. They must reflect the library's objectives, be reasonable, flexible, well communicated, and thoroughly explained, and they must be implemented fairly and consistently through the development of appropriate rules and procedures.

10

Censorship

- *What should a library do before a complaint is lodged against library materials?*
- *What should a library selection policy contain?*
- *How often are challenges to library materials successful?*
- *Why is it important to have a policy for reconsideration?*

Censorship is always a "hot" topic with librarians. They worry that their increasing inability to buy everything because of ever-tightening fiscal constraints may appear to be censorship on their part. They are warned regularly by professional publications that incidents of censorship by special interest groups and individuals are increasing every year.

Censorship is a very important issue for library patrons. Generally, it is a library user or the parent of a library user who makes a complaint about library material. And, of course, users certainly have the right to file complaints.

On the other hand, librarians should protect the right of other library users to have access to the material in question. People disagree about what is and is not appropriate material for library shelves. But libraries do not insist that patrons use or take out materials that they find objectionable; the material is there to be used freely by those who *do* find it appropriate for their needs or interests.

Two types of libraries—public and school libraries—are particularly vulnerable to attacks on library materials. Children's departments in public libraries are most apt to find their materials under scrutiny, while school libraries also find that protection of children is the main interest of those who complain about what is on the shelf. There are also challenges to adult materials.

Parents are rightly concerned with what their own children read, hear, and view, but they have no right to prevent access for other children. Public library circulation policies often state that parents or guardians are responsible for the materials borrowed by children. But the availability of materials that one parent finds suitable for his or her child does not mean that other parents or guardians will agree that the material is appropriate for their children. If the parent or guardian who objects to a particular book or audiovisual tries to have the item removed from the collection, the issue can cause a great deal of dissension and emotional wear and tear. There are many cases where either a parent or an organized group has tried to have material removed from a public or school library.

While the censors object most frequently to juvenile materials, there are challenges to adult materials as well, usually on religious, ethnic, sexual, or idealogical grounds.

Who Does the Challenging and What Do They Challenge?

Individuals or groups may initiate the challenge to a library book, video, audio, or even a program such as a film series. It is commonplace for challenges to involve all age levels of children's books.

There are a number of titles that have been challenged repeatedly. One of the most challenged publications over the past three years is the picture book *Daddy's Roommate*. In it, a young boy tells the story of his life with his father, after his mother and father divorce, and his father's male roommate. The pictures and text make it clear, to an adult, that the relationship between the two men is a homosexual one. The book pictures the boy and the men at a number of routine household tasks such as cleaning and grocery shopping. The illustrations include one where the men are in bed together with the child standing beside the bed. This book has been attacked a number of times. Some complaintants have requested its removal from the library's shelves, while others have sought reclassification to adult or "parenting" collections.

Some religious groups claim that *Daddy's Roommate* condones homosexuality as a lifestyle. Others have stated that the book indicates that homosexuality is normal but the Bible clearly condemns it. Individuals and groups have called the book's subject matter inappropriate for young children. There is a genuine concern on the part of the parents and groups that have lodged these objections. In school systems such as New York City's, where the book had been selected as part of the reading package to introduce children to different cultures and lifestyles, there has been so much controversy that school administrators have backed off from requiring the book to be read.[1] *Daddy's Roommate*, has been challenged many times in public libraries. Although it has usually withstood the challenges, it continues to be a title that "walks." That is, people who cannot get it officially removed from the shelves have taken to physically removing the book from the library—either by checking it out and "losing" it or by taking it without checking it out.

According to the ALA's Office for Intellectual Freedom, the ten most challenged books for the period September 1, 1990 through December 31, 1994 were[2]:

Rank	Title	Author	No. of challenges
1	*Daddy's Roommate*	Michael Willhoite	80
2	*Impressions Reading Series*	Harcourt Brace Jovanovich	44
3	*More Scary Stories to Tell in the Dark*	Alvin Schwartz	33
4	*Heather Has Two Mommies*	Leslea Newman	29
4	*Scary Stories to Tell in the Dark*	Alvin Schwartz	29
5	*Bridge to Terabithia*	Katherine Patterson	26
6	*Sex*	Madonna	25
7	*Forever*	Judy Blume	21
8	*The Adventures of Huckleberry Finn*	Mark Twain	20
8	*Of Mice and Men*	John Steinbeck	20

Two organizations that monitor censorship incidents, the Office for Intellectual Freedom of the American Library Association and People for the American Way, determined that 41 percent of the challenges to library books were successful during the 1992–93 school year.[3] These organizations have ascertained that conservative groups, some of them part of the religious right, have come to be a powerful part of the movement to ferret out materials that they feel teach the wrong values, contain vulgar words, deal with sensitive subjects, or depict violence. These groups often point out that tax money pays for the materials in question and therefore citizens should have a active part in determining what is being purchased.

While young people's materials are commonly the focus of complaints, adult materials also sometimes draw the ire of patrons, either in and of themselves or because they are available to children in unrestricted library collections. These materials may even be targeted by those who are labeled liberals and progressives. For example, feminists may object to sexist images or language or African Americans may take umbrage when all of the black characters in a work are portrayed as criminals or when racial epithets are part of books like *The Adventures of Huckleberry Finn*. Italian Americans point out that their counterparts in literature are often employed as gangsters. Other groups have similar complaints.

The February 15, 1992, issue of *Library Journal* carried a summary of early results of the National Opinion Poll on Library Issues. This telephone survey of a national sample of 1,181 people found that on the issue of censorship, librarians and the library public are at odds. Almost 70 percent of the people surveyed believed that some materials, such as *Playboy*, *Penthouse*, and books on committing suicide, shouldn't be in libraries at all. Almost half of those surveyed felt that sexually explicit audiovisuals did not belong in libraries. While recognizing strong public concern that parents be the final authority on what their children read, hear, and view, intellectual freedom advocates ask why any one group should impose its opinions and views on *all* the children of a class, school, or community. Librarians, on the other hand, are educated to select and provide a wide range of materials on all sides of an issue for their clientele using professional selection tools and following a selection policy. They feel that inviting the public into the selection process opens the door to special interests and hidden agendas. How would a library choose participants for the selection process from the user pool?

Library publications continually report on complaints about juvenile and adult materials in libraries. But reading about such an incident and living through one are, without doubt, quite different experiences. There are ways, though, to prepare for a patron complaint about library materials.

WHEN A COMPLAINT IS LODGED AGAINST LIBRARY MATERIALS

Several actions must be taken before a complaint occurs. First, a selection policy should be in place that guides the staff in choosing materials for the collection. The policy may state that standard review media will be employed in this selection process or it may actually name the publications. If the titles are part of the document, an annual review must be done to make sure that it includes any new reviewing tools that have been chosen. This is particularly true in the realm of technology.

Staff members who select in a particular subject area should note where reviews appeared for works chosen for the collection. If there are several titles on a particular subject with good reviews, but only one can be purchased, the rationale for the item chosen might be recorded for future reference. It is important to note, however, that sometimes materials that have received consistently poor reviews may nevertheless be appropriate and necessary selections for a library collection due to public curiosity, interest, demand, or lack of other materials on the subject.

In public libraries, the *New York Times* or *Publishers Weekly* best-seller lists are sometimes used as the rationale for materials purchases. Because public library users often go directly to the new books section to find reading matter, these best-seller lists can be used to choose the latest materials that frequent users seek. Another factor in choosing materials for a public library is requests from the public. If several patrons mention a title they would like to read, or if there are several interlibrary loan requests for a particular title, the library often purchases the item for the collection. Sometimes an author appears on television, sparking patron interest and leading to requests for a title.

The selection policy should state that the library carries materials that reflect a range of points of view. For example, materials that deal with human sexuality might be represented by medical, religious, feminist, and other points of view. Rational people can see that the library is attempting to cover the topic in a broad way, without advocating which viewpoint is correct or which book patrons should read. Patrons might wish to read several works to make up their own minds on this or any other issue. That is what libraries do best—provide information without judging the merits of the opinions expressed.

School boards are in a particularly interesting position with regard to attempts at censorship of library materials. While school boards remain the primary controllers of local systems, there have been some indicators that if a school board removes challenged material from a school library without due process or because it seeks to suppress information or ideas with which it disagrees, it may be violating the students' right to access to information. In 1973, the U.S. Supreme Court sided with junior and senior high school students who claimed that the removal of several books from the school library violated their First Amendment rights. That case,

Pico, et al. v. *Board of Education, Island Trees (New York) Union Free School District 26*, left the issue of exactly how much power school boards have in the matter of book removal up in the air. District, circuit, and state courts have generally ruled that the operation of the school system, including the acquisition and removal of library materials, is part of a school board's responsibility, best left to the judgment of the members as representatives of the community's values. But the suppression of ideas merely because members of the school board disagree with them or find them offensive has been consistently condemned. The Supreme Court's majority opinion in this case is reprinted in Appendix A.

Pico and other findings indicate that school systems need carefully developed selection policies with strong rationales for including a range of materials on all sides of an issue. Certainly at the high school level students are approaching adulthood and need training in thinking critically. They need to be able to read materials that contain varying opinions and ideas, including those that are "out of sync" with those of their parents. Some if not all of the materials will have both advocates and critics. Each side has a right to an opinion. But the issue is whether or not those who find the material offensive or contrary to their beliefs have the right to deprive others of access to the materials.

Once a selection policy is in place, a procedure for the reconsideration of materials should also be developed. The procedure should respect the right of individuals to object to books or other materials and should mandate an objective process for examining the situation and for making a considered decision about the disposition of the complaint. It should specify the steps to be followed by the institution and its officials as well as by the person making the complaint. Complaint forms are an important part of this procedure, with the complainant asked to read the whole work and cite specific pages and passages in context. As part of the policy for reconsideration, there should be a procedure for forming a committee with wide representation from the library's governing authority, library administration, library staff, professionals from outside the institution and possibly the library friends, students, parents, and other community representatives. The committee members should have training in the area of intellectual freedom. A review of pertinent court cases can also be helpful. The advice of a qualified attorney is always desirable in staying within the law while protecting the rights of all patrons.

Another part of the process for dealing with censorship is to keep the library's public well informed about what is purchased or added through gifts to the library's collection. Often, just the fact that the library does not require the reading of any material by any reader of any age is worth stating. The public often misconstrues selection of materials as an endorsement by the library of the ideas expressed. The community should be informed that this is not the case—the library is a neutral provider of information from various points of view. Reminding parents that it is their responsibility to monitor their children's borrowing and reading habits is worthwhile, too. Libraries are still viewed by many as a safe haven for their children, and finding material on the library shelf that offends a parent's sensibilities can come as a shock, almost an insult, that can lead to overreaction.

On the other hand, library literature contains a number of warnings about organized efforts on the part of some groups to target library materials. Some people predict that there will be the same kind of effort to censor library materials as there is to close abortion clinics. Controversial topics expected to be targeted include sex, vulgar language, sexual preference, satanism, violence, and religious matters.

Although the controversy that is part of a request for reconsideration can be stressful, librarians can take heart from the fact that with solid policies and procedures in place, the airing of the pros and cons presented by both sides in the process can be a healthy exercise in democracy. Such incidents often increase understanding of libraries and strengthen the position of the library in the community or the school system. People need to realize that the library is a resource for acquiring information on all sides of an issue. Often the complainant discovers that his or her point of view is already represented among the materials on a particular topic. It may be easier then for that individual to understand why it is fair to have other points of view in the collection as well, although all too often such complainants believe that their view is the only valid one.

WHERE TO FIND INFORMATION AND HELP

The American Library Association's *Intellectual Freedom Manual,* compiled by the ALA Office for Intellectual Freedom, is filled with good advice about preparing for challenges to library materials. It suggests a series of actions to take before, during, and after a complaint. It is an essential tool in the area of censorship.

The office itself offers a case support service, providing direct advice and assistance in connection with specific challenges. When a complaint is received, the office should be contacted to report the incident and seek help, if needed. It can be reached at 1-800-545-2433, ext. 4223.

The Public Library Association, a division of the American Library Association, has developed the *PLA Handbook for Writers of Public Library Policies*. This is another tool that can provide invaluable assistance for policy writers—even those in other than public libraries.

Additionally, there is much written on an ongoing basis about the topic of censorship and how to handle it. For example, in her article "Is Sex Safe in Your Library?: How to Fight Censorship" Martha Cornog suggests 11 ways to answer a censor. While she concentrates on books that are potential problems because of their sexual content, her suggestions are worth studying for application to objections of other types.[4]

Popular novelist and intellectual freedom advocate Richard Peck recommends publicizing the fact that methods are in place to deal with book challenges. He further advocates firm handling of the complaint.[5]

These are just a few of the many articles, books, and human resources available to help in determining the best approach in a given situation. Each library must decide on its own procedure to employ when someone raises an objection to an item in the collection. No two incidents are exactly the same. But, by using the available resources to construct a policy and procedure tailored to the particular institution, a library will be prepared to deal with complaints in a legal, orderly, consistent, and reasonable way. All policies and procedures must be reviewed frequently to maintain currency with and to anticipate new developments in the library's mission, goals, and objectives. This is as true for reconsideration policies and procedures as it is for those on other subjects.

ENDNOTES

1. Lacayo, Richard, "Jack and Jack and Jill and Jill." *Time*, 12 December 1992, 52.
2. ALA Office for Intellectual Freedom, "OIF Censorship Debate" (Unpublished, 1995), 7.
3. "41% of Censorship Attempts Successful, News Report Says," *School Library Journal* 39 (October 1993), 10.
4. Martha Cornog, "Is Sex Safe in Your Library?" *Library Journal* vol. no. (13 August 1993), 43.
5. Richard Peck, "The Great Library-Shelf Witch Hunt," *Booklist* vol. no. (1 January 1992), 816.

11
Patron Questions and Answers

- *How should library staffs, administrators, and members of a governing board respond to patron questions about library rules and regulations?*

Library administrators, governing boards, and staff members are often asked questions about library rules and regulations. It is important to explain these library rules properly as well as the legal reasoning behind them. Below are some of these types of questions, along with suggested answers that may help a library patron understand the reasons for regulations.

Question 1: Do I have a legal right to attend my public library's board of trustees meetings?
It depends on the status of your public library. In some states, the local public library is really a private entity. In such cases, the state's freedom of information law and/or open meeting law, which usually mandates that the public can attend such meetings, may not obtain because the meetings are private. However, public library boards are usually pleased to see citizen interest and welcome anyone who wishes to observe.

Remember though, even in states where the library is a public service and subject to the state's "sunshine" laws, there are portions of some meetings—when the board is dealing with personnel issues or with bidding limits for building alterations, for example—that are legally closed to anyone but board members.

Question 2: My public library is in a 100-year old building that was enlarged and modernized about 25 years ago. There are a num-

ber of front steps, making it inaccessible to persons with certain disabilities. There is not enough space in the area of the steps to install a ramp. The library does have a bookmobile, which visits shut-ins and other persons who cannot get to the library. Does that satisfy the requirements of the Americans with Disabilities Act?

Assuming that your library is part of county or local government, you need to know that a public entity must ensure that individuals with disabilities are not excluded from services, programs, and activities because existing buildings are inaccessible. A state or local government's programs, when viewed in their entirety, must be readily accessible to and usable by individuals with disabilities. This standard, known as " program accessibility," applies to facilities that existed on January 26, 1992. Public entities do not necessarily have to make *each* of their existing facilities accessible. They may provide program accessibility by a number of methods including alteration of existing facilities, acquisition or construction of additional facilities, relocation of a service or program to an accessible facility, or provision of services at alternative accessible sites.

Bookmobiles, volunteers, or library personnel that deliver materials to people with mobility problems are viable alternatives to building alterations when alterations are extremely costly or impossible because of the site. Some libraries provide books by mail, with postage paid by the library. The federal government sponsors a program for blind and physically-handicapped persons that provides both recorded materials and players free through the mail. For those who prefer them, braille books are also available.

Relocating library programs such as book discussion groups to space that is accessible to all is also an acceptable alternative.

Question 3: My public library's open stacks are located on upper floors having no elevator. The stairs are too narrow to install a lift, and the cost of an elevator, if there were room for one, is prohibitive. This is a problem for people in wheelchairs. What can be done?

The law allows for alternative provision of services. In this case, library staff may retrieve books for patrons who use wheelchairs, as long as that service is available during the library's operating hours.

Question 4: As the director of the local public library, I want a policy on sexual harassment developed and placed in our policy manual. My library board says it is not necessary because all the staff members are women. Are they right?

No. Tell the board that sexual harassment policies include provisions for dealing with harrassment whether it is demonstrated by staff members, patrons, board members, vendors or anyone else. The library may also employ male staff members in the future. There has already been one well-publicized case of same-sex sexual harassment charges being lodged against a female professor. Look through the literature and bring a few articles about the issue of sexual harassment to the next board meeting. It will serve to raise consciousness on a current topic.

Question 5: I am a member of a small group of people who are in the process of establishing a new church in our community. We want to have organizational meetings in the public library's community room. When I inquired about scheduling some meetings there, the staff told me that the library didn't allow religious groups to meet there. We found a temporary place, but the library's space is much nicer. Why are we shut out?

You may not have to be. It depends on the rules of use for the library's meeting space. What kind of groups are allowed, according to the rules? Often, only nonprofit local groups are allowed. You are probably in that category. If there is a broad range of groups allowed to meet there—not just municipal departments, for example—you may have a right to do so. Even though the library itself is a limited public forum where people are expected to come for certain purposes, its meeting rooms may be open to all community groups, regardless of the groups' purpose. Ask the library staff to get an opinion on this issue from the town attorney. You may be pleasantly surprised with the outcome.

Question 6: I am a senior citizen who does volunteer work at the library. I have an interest in local history. There is a book on the history of our town in the history room that I would like for my collection. I can't afford to buy one, although there are still a few for sale from the local historical society at a price of $57.50. I thought that I would make a copy on the library's copy machine by doing a few pages a week. I get to use the key for the copier so I could do it at no cost. When I told one of the circulation staff about my plan, she said that I would be breaking the law. I don't believe that. What harm would there be in what I plan to do?

The staff member was trying to warn you that whoever owns the copyright on the book you want to copy might be able to sue you for copyright infringement if you carry out your plan. Under the copyright laws of the United States, copying a complete work is prohibited, except in certain, narrowly defined circumstances. Your situation does not fit those circumstances. Therefore, you should not do the copying unless and until you seek and receive permission from the copyright holder. In other words, you should write to the local historical society, explain your circumstances, and seek written permission to do the copying you describe. It may be sympathetic and allow it. On the other hand, it may not. Don't do it without permission.

Question 7: I have two small children who attend the public library's story hours and who always want to take out books on the days we go there. There are a lot of really wonderful books on the shelves, but there are also some that I think are inappropriate for young children. For example, I don't think that the book called Where the Wild Things Are *by Maurice Sendak should be there—it must cause nightmares for any child who reads it. What can I do to eliminate this book from the library?*

Your library undoubtedly has a policy for the reconsideration of material. If you wish to make a formal complaint about the book, ask the staff for a complaint form and for any instructions to go with it. Libraries always take seriously any person's opinion on a library resource. This does not mean, however, that the library will remove the material. It simply means that it will review the material as to its suitability for the collection. If it meets the library's collection criteria, it will remain in the library. If that happens, remember that a wide range of people with many opinions use the library. What one person considers wonderful, another person may abhor. That does not mean that the item should not be in the library. It does mean that if you find a work unsuitable for either you or your children, you needn't borrow it.

Question 8: I think of my public library as a place not only where my children enjoy themselves but also where they are very safe. Now our library has instituted a policy that says my children can't be left there alone. I like to drop them off there on Saturday morning—they are seven- and nine-year old girls—when I go grocery shopping and pick them up after I'm through. Usually, I'm at the store for an hour to an hour-and-a-half. The children's librarian gave the girls a copy of this new policy yesterday. I don't see any harm in what I've been doing. The girls hate going to the store with me. They are very happy at the library. Can the library make rules like this? I thought it was a public institution. And my taxes pay for this service.

Your attitude that the public library is a safe place to leave young children unattended is a common one. Librarians wish that they felt it was a safe place for them, too. But, unfortunately, that is not the case. The library is a public place where all kinds of people enter—wonderful people and not-so-wonderful ones, too. The library staff cannot possibly take on the responsibility for the safety of your children.

Court cases have determined that a public library is a limited public forum where people may go for the specific purposes of using library materials and services. The courts have said that public libraries may make policies and rules for use of the library. One of the policies that libraries usually put in place is one dealing with unattended children of specific ages. More and more libraries have found it necessary to do this. Please understand that it is for the safety of the children.

Question 9: Our library has a poetry discussion group. There are between a dozen and twenty people in attendance every two weeks. The library has a limited number of the anthologies that contain our poem of the week. I have suggested that the library staff make twenty copies of the week's poem and put them on the information desk for the people in the group. The librarians say that the copyright law won't allow that. I think they just don't want to make the copies.

Perhaps the staff members didn't give you the section number of the copyright law that would help you discover that they are right. Take a look at the United States Code, Section 107 (Fair Use), and you'll see that the staff is being careful to stay within the law.

As an individual, you may be entitled to make a copy for yourself under this section of the law. You need to read the section and decide for yourself. However, it is clear that under this section and the one following, Section 108, it would not be proper for the library to make and disseminate twenty copies of the poem being discussed unless permission had been granted in writing by the copyright holder for such an action.

Question 10: I am embarrassed when I visit the library and have to ask for the key to the rest room. This is especially true because I am on medication that causes me to need to use the facility more frequently than average. Can the library legally lock up the rest rooms?

Yes, the library can keep the rest rooms locked if there is reason to believe that this is safer for all patrons. Libraries realized some time ago that their rest rooms must be policed to assure that inappropriate or illegal activities are not conducted there. People who contemplate such activities are less likely to carry them out once they realize their use of the facility is not anonymous.

Question 11: Last week the book I wanted to borrow from the library was out. Because I had a paper due, I needed to look up some material in it quickly. I asked the library to give me the name of the person who had the book so I could call him or her to see if I could use the book for a couple of days. The staff wouldn't do that, saying that it's priviliged information. I can't believe that anyone would care if someone knew he or she had a library book.

Believe it. Most states have laws that protect the confidentiality of library records. This is especially true of the connection between library patrons and the materials that they borrow. What a person reads is a private matter. In some states, what questions patrons ask in a library, what materials they use while in the facility, and what materials they request (whether or not they actually receive them) are also confidential. If there is a justifiable reason for law enforcement personnel to get the information, they can obtain it only by subpoena.

Question 12: My public library is open on Sundays, the only day of the week that I am able to get to it. The library recently posted a notice that it would be closed on Easter Sunday. Why is the library closing on a religious holiday? Isn't there supposed to be a separation between church and state?

Library staff members have an identified series of holidays that are either part of a negotiated labor contract or part of a personnel manual or handbook. Apparently, your library has included Easter Sunday as part of the agreed-upon days for closing, probably anticipating low use. Closing on Easter Sunday was not intended to be an endorsement of that holiday. There is no law against the library closing on that particular Sunday. However, you certainly have the right to make your objections to the closing known to library administrators.

Question 13: A library regulation requires that staff members placed on suspension may not to come to the library until notified otherwise. Doesn't this violate the staff member's First Amendment rights?

No. The library is a limited public forum. The library may regulate public access as long as it is reasonable and not an effort to suppress a speaker's point of view. Libraries should not be required to provide access to a disgruntled employee who may pose a threat or to one who, for whatever reason, has been suspended from duty for violating job rules. If a barred employee needs to enter the library for some reason, the library can allow an escorted entry for a reasonable period of time.

Question 14: The rules at my library prohibit anyone using the library who has offensive body odor. What if such a person just wanted to read a book and be left alone? Could the library just throw him or her out? Don't homeless people also have rights?

Libraries try to treat *all* library patrons fairly. If the body odor of a library user is so offensive that it causes discomfort for other users, the library must act to correct the situation. Libraries may make rules that require an offender to be expelled. These rules must be applied fairly and evenhandedly.

Your question implies that the person with the offensive body odor is homeless. Homeless people do have rights, but not greater rights than the library's other patrons. The library staff can help homeless people by referring them to the proper agencies for shelter, food, clothing, and bathing facilities.

Appendix A

BOARD OF EDUCATION V. PICO

Pico was the first (school) library censorship case taken up by the U.S. Supreme Court. It is also the only case so far where the Court has considered the constitutional right to receive information and ideas in a library setting. Pico *also played an important part in development of that constitutional right. Set forth below is the majority opinion of the Court.* Pico *actually had seven separate opinions.*

Board of Education, Island Trees Union Free School District No. 26, et al. v. Pico, by his next Friend Pico, et al.

Argued March 2, 1982
Decided June 25, 1982
JUSTICE BRENNAN announced the judgment of the Court and delivered an opinion, in which JUSTICE MARSHALL and JUSTICE STEVENS joined, and in which JUSTICE BLACKMUN joined except for Part II-A-(1).

The principal question presented is whether the First Amendment imposes limitations upon the exercise by a local school board of its discretion to remove library books from high school and junior high school libraries.

I

Petitioners are the Board of Education of the Island Trees Union Free School District No. 26, in New York, and Richard Ahrens, Frank Martin, Christina Fasulo, Patrick Hughes, Richard Melchers, Richard Michaels, and Louis Nessim. When this suit was brought, Ahrens was the President of the Board, Martin was the Vice President, and the remaining petitioners were Board members. The Board is a state agency charged with responsibility for the operation and administration of the public schools within the Island Trees School District, including the Island Trees High School and Island Trees Memorial Junior High School. Respondents are Steven Pico, Jacqueline Gold, Glenn Yarris, Russell Rieger, and Paul Sochinski. When this suit was brought, Pico, Gold, Yarris, and Rieger were students at the High School, and Sochinski was a student at the Junior High School.

In September, 1975, petitioners Ahrens, Martin, and Hughes attended a conference sponsored by Parents of New York United (PONYU), a politically conservative organization of parents concerned about education legislation in the State of New York. At the conference, these petitioners obtained lists of books described by Ahrens as "objectionable," App. 22, and by Martin as "improper fare for school students," *id.* at 101. It was later determined that the High School library contained nine of the listed books, and that another listed book was in the Junior High School library. In February, 1976, at a meeting with the Superintendent of Schools and the Principals of the High School and Junior High School, the Board gave an "unofficial direction" that the listed books be removed from the library shelves and delivered to the Board's offices so that Board members could read them. When this directive was carried out, it became publicized, and the Board issued a press release justifying its action. It characterized the removed books as "anti-American, anti-Christian, anti-Sem[i]tic, and just plain filthy," and concluded that "[i]t is our duty, our moral obligation, to protect the children in our schools from this moral danger as surely as from physical and medical dangers." 474 F.Supp. 387, 390 (EDNY 1979).

A short time later, the Board appointed a "Book Review Committee," consisting of four Island Trees parents and four members of the Island Trees schools staff, to read the listed books and to recommend to the Board whether the books should be retained, taking into account the books' "educational suitability," "good taste," "relevance," and "appropriateness to age and grade level." In July, the Committee made its final report to the Board, recommending that five of the listed books be retained and that two others be removed from the school libraries. As for the remaining four books, the Committee could not agree on two, took no position on one, and recommended that the last book be made available to students only with parental approval. The Board substantially rejected the Committee's report later that month, deciding that only one book should be returned to the High School library without restriction, that another should be made available subject to parental approval but that the remaining nine books should "be removed from elementary and secondary libraries and [from] use in the curriculum." *Id.* at 391. The Board gave no reasons for rejecting the recommendations of the Committee that it had appointed.

Respondents reacted to the Board's decision by bringing the present action under 42 U.S.C. sec. 1983 in the United States District Court for the Eastern District of New York. They alleged that petitioners had:

> "ordered the removal of the books from school libraries and proscribed their use in the curriculum because particular passages in the books offended their social, political and moral tastes, and not because the books, taken as a whole, were lacking in educational value." App. 4.

Respondents claimed that the Board's actions denied them their rights under the First Amendment. They asked the court for a declaration that the Board's actions were unconstitutional, and for preliminary and permanent injunctive relief ordering the Board to return the nine books to the school libraries and to refrain from interfering with the use of those books in the schools' curricula. *Id.* at 5–6.

The District Court granted summary judgment in favor of petitioners. 474 F.Supp. 387 (1979). In the court's view, "the parties substantially agree[d] about the motivation behind the board's actions," *id.* at 391—namely, that

> "the board acted not on religious principles, but on its conservative educational philosophy, and on its belief that the nine books removed from the school library and curriculum were irrelevant, vulgar, immoral, and in bad taste, making them educationally unsuitable for the district's junior and senior high school students." *Id.* at 392.

With this factual premise as its background, the court rejected respondents' contention that their First Amendment rights had been infringed by the Board's actions. Noting that statutes, history, and precedent had vested local school boards with a broad discretion to formulate educational policy, the court concluded that it should not intervene in "'the daily operations of school systems'" unless "'basic constitutional values'" were "'sharply implicate[d],'" and determined that the conditions for such intervention did not exist in the present case. Acknowledging that the "removal [of the books] . . . clearly was content-based," the court nevertheless found no constitutional violation of the requisite magnitude:

> "The board has restricted access only to certain books which the board

believed to be, in essence, vulgar. While removal of such books from a
school library may . . . reflect a misguided educational philosophy, it does
not constitute a sharp and direct infringement of any first amendment
right." *Id.* at 397.

A three-judge panel of the United States Court of Appeals for
the Second Circuit reversed the judgment of the District Court,
and remanded the action for a trial on respondents' allegations.
638 F.2d 404 (1980). Each judge on the panel filed a separate opinion. Delivering the judgment of the court, Judge Sifton treated the
case as involving "an unusual and irregular intervention in the
school libraries' operations by persons not routinely concerned with
such matters," and concluded that petitioners were obliged to demonstrate a reasonable basis for interfering with respondents' First
Amendment rights. *Id.* at 414–415. He then determined that, at
least at the summary judgment stage, petitioners had not offered
sufficient justification for their action, and concluded that respondents should have . . . been offered an opportunity to persuade a
finder of fact that the ostensible justifications for [petitioners']
actions . . . were simply pretexts for the suppression of free speech."
Id. at 417. Judge Newman concurred in the result. *Id.* at 432–438.
He viewed the case as turning on the contested factual issue of
whether petitioners' removal decision was motivated by a justifiable desire to remove books containing vulgarities and sexual ex-
plicitness, or rather by an impermissible desire to suppress ideas.
Id. at 861. We granted certiorari, 454 U.S. 891 (1981).

II

We emphasize at the outset the limited nature of the substantive question presented by the case before us. Our precedents have
long recognized certain constitutional limits upon the power of the
State to control even the curriculum and classroom. For example,
Meyer v. *Nebraska*, 262 U.S. 390 (1923), struck down a state law
that forbade the teaching of modern foreign languages in public
and private schools, and *Epperson* v. *Arkansas*, 393 U.S. 97 (1968),
declared unconstitutional a state law that prohibited the teaching
of the Darwinian theory of evolution in any state-supported school.
But the current action does not require us to reenter this difficult
terrain, which *Meyer* and *Epperson* traversed without apparent
misgiving. For as this case is presented to us, it does not involve
textbooks, or indeed any books that Island Trees students would
be required to read. Respondents do not seek in this Court to impose limitations upon their school Board's discretion to prescribe
the curricula of the Island Trees schools. On the contrary, the only

books at issue in this case are *library* books, books that, by their nature, are optional, rather than required, reading. Our adjudication of the present case thus does not intrude into the classroom, or into the compulsory courses taught there. Furthermore, even as to library books, the action before us does not involve the *acquisition* of books. Respondents have not sought to compel their school Board to add to the school library shelves any books that students desire to read. Rather, the only action challenged in this case is the *removal* from school libraries of books originally placed there by the school authorities, or without objection from them.

The substantive question before us is still further constrained by the procedural posture of this case. Petitioners were granted summary judgment by the District Court. The Court of Appeals reversed that judgment, and remanded the action for a trial on the merits of respondents' claims. We can reverse the judgment of the Court of Appeals, and grant petitioners' request for reinstatement of the summary judgment in their favor, only if we determine that "there is no genuine issue as to any material fact," and that petitioners are "entitled to a judgment as a matter of law." Fed.Rule Civ.Proc. 56(c). In making our determination, any doubt as to the existence of a genuine issue of material fact must be resolved against petitioners as the moving party. *Adickes* v. *S. H. Kress & Co.*, 398 U.S. 144, 157–159 (1970). Furthermore, [o]n summary judgment the inferences to be drawn from the underlying facts contained in [the affidavits, attached exhibits, and depositions submitted below] must be viewed in the light most favorable to the party opposing the motion. *United States* v. *Diebold, Inc.*, 369 U.S. 654, 655 (1962).

In sum, the issue before us in this case is a narrow one, both substantively and procedurally. It may best be restated as two distinct questions. First, does the First Amendment impose *any* limitations upon the discretion of petitioners to remove library books from the Island Trees High School and Junior High School? Second, if so, do the affidavits and other evidentiary materials before the District Court, construed most favorably to respondents, raise a genuine issue of fact whether petitioners might have exceeded those limitations? If we answer either of these questions in the negative, then we must reverse the judgment of the Court of Appeals and reinstate the District Court's summary judgment for petitioners. If we answer both questions in the affirmative, then we must affirm the judgment below. We examine these questions in turn.

A

(1)

The Court has long recognized that local school boards have broad discretion in the management of school affairs. See, e.g., *Meyer* v. *Nebraska*, supra, at 402; *Pierce* v. *Society of Sisters*, 268 U.S. 510, 534 (1925). *Epperson* v. *Arkansas*, supra, at 104, reaffirmed that, by and large, "public education in our Nation is committed to the control of state and local authorities," and that federal courts should not ordinarily "intervene in the resolution of conflicts which arise in the daily operation of school systems." *Tinker* v. *Des Moines School Dist.*, 393 U.S. 503, 507 (1969), noted that we have "repeatedly emphasized . . . the comprehensive authority of the States and of school officials . . . to prescribe and control conduct in the schools." We have also acknowledged that public schools are vitally important "in the preparation of individuals for participation as citizens," and as vehicles for "inculcating fundamental values necessary to the maintenance of a democratic political system." *Ambach* v. *Norwick*, 441 U.S. 68, 777 (1979). We are therefore in full agreement with petitioners that local school boards must be permitted "to establish and apply their curriculum in such a way as to transmit community values," and that "there is a legitimate and substantial community interest in promoting respect for authority and traditional values be they social, moral, or political." Brief for Petitioners 10.

At the same time, however, we have necessarily recognized that the discretion of the States and local school boards in matters of education must be exercised in a manner that comports with the transcendent imperatives of the First Amendment. In *West Virginia Board of Education* v. *Barnette*, 319 U.S. 624 (1943), we held that, under the First Amendment, a student in a public school could not be compelled to salute the flag. We reasoned:

> Boards of Education . . . have, of course, important, delicate, and highly discretionary functions, but none that they may not perform within the limits of the Bill of Rights. That they are educating the young for citizenship is reason for scrupulous protection of Constitutional freedoms of the individual, if we are not to strangle the free mind at its source and teach youth to discount important principles of our government as mere platitudes. *Id.* at 637.

Later cases have consistently followed this rationale. Thus, *Epperson* v. *Arkansas* invalidated a State's anti-evolution statute as violative of the Establishment Clause, and reaffirmed the duty of federal courts to apply the First Amendment's mandate in our educational system where essential to safeguard the fundamental values of freedom of speech and inquiry. 393 U.S. at 104. And *Tinker v. Des Moines School Dist.,* supra, held that a local school board had infringed the free speech rights of high school and junior high school students by suspending them from school for wearing black armbands in class as a protest against the Government's policy in Vietnam; we stated there that the "comprehensive authority... of school officials" must be exercised "consistent with fundamental constitutional safeguards." 393 U.S. at 507. In sum, students do not "shed their constitutional rights to freedom of speech or expression at the schoolhouse gate," *id.* at 506, and therefore local school boards must discharge their "important, delicate, and highly discretionary functions" within the limits and constraints of the First Amendment.

The nature of students' First Amendment rights in the context of this case requires further examination. *West Virginia Board of Education* v. *Barnette,* supra, is instructive. There the Court held that students' liberty of conscience could not be infringed in the name of "national unity" or "patriotism." 319 U.S. at 640–641. We explained that

> the action of the local authorities in compelling the flag salute and pledge transcends constitutional limitations on their power and invades the sphere of intellect and spirit which it is the purpose of the First Amendment to our Constitution to reserve from all official control. *Id.* at 642.

Similarly, *Tinker* v. *Des Moines School Dist.*, supra, held that students' rights to freedom of expression of their political views could not be abridged by reliance upon an "undifferentiated fear or apprehension of disturbance" arising from such expression:

> Any departure from absolute regimentation may cause trouble. Any variation from the majority's opinion may inspire fear. Any word spoken, in class, in the lunchroom, or on the campus, that deviates from the views of another person may start an argument or cause a disturbance. But our Constitution says we must take this risk, Terminiello v. Chicago, 337 U.S. 1 (1949); and our history says that it is this sort of hazardous freedom—this kind of openness—that is the basis of our national strength and of the independence and vigor of Americans who grow up and live in this ... often disputatious society. 393 U.S. at 508-509.

In short, "First Amendment rights, applied in light of the special characteristics of the school environment, are available to ... students. *Id.* at 506.

Of course, courts should not "intervene in the resolution of conflicts which arise in the daily operation of school systems" unless "basic constitutional values" are "directly and sharply implicate[d]" in those conflicts. *Epperson* v. *Arkansas*, 393 U.S. at 104. But we think that the First Amendment rights of students may be directly and sharply implicated by the removal of books from the shelves of a school library. Our precedents have focused not only on the role of the First Amendment in fostering individual self-expression, but also on its role in affording the public access to discussion, debate, and the dissemination of information and ideas. *First National Bank of Boston* v. *Bellotti*, 435 U.S. 765, 783 (1978). And we have recognized that "the State may not, consistently with the spirit of the First Amendment, contract the spectrum of available knowledge." *Griswold* v. *Connecticut*, 381 U.S. 479, 482 (1965). In keeping with this principle, we have held that, in a variety of contexts, "the Constitution protects the right to receive information and ideas." *Stanley* v. *Georgia*, 394 U.S. 557, 564 (1969); see *Kleindienst* v. *Mandel*, 408 U.S. 753, 762–763 (1972) (citing cases). This right is an inherent corollary of the rights of free speech and press that are explicitly guaranteed by the Constitution, in two senses. First, the right to receive ideas follows ineluctably from the *sender's* First Amendment right to send them: "The right of freedom of speech and press . . . embraces the right to distribute literature, and necessarily protects the right to receive it." *Martin* v. *Struthers*, 319 U.S. 141, 143 (1943) (citation omitted).

The dissemination of ideas can accomplish nothing if otherwise willing addressees are not free to receive and consider them. It would be a barren marketplace of ideas that had only sellers, and no buyers. *Lamont* v. *Postmaster General*, 381 U.S. 301, 308 (1965) (BRENNAN, J., concurring).

More importantly, the right to receive ideas is a necessary predicate to the *recipient's* meaningful exercise of his own rights of speech, press, and political freedom. Madison admonished us:

A popular Government, without popular information, or the means of acquiring it, is but a Prologue to a Farce or a Tragedy, or perhaps both. Knowledge will forever govern ignorance, and a people who mean to be their own Governors must arm themselves with the power which knowledge gives. 9 Writings of James Madison 103 (G. Hunt ed.1910)

As we recognized in *Tinker*, students too are beneficiaries of this principle:

In our system, students may not be regarded as closed-circuit recipients of only that which the State chooses to communicate. . . . [S]chool officials cannot suppress 'expressions of feeling with which they do not wish to contend.' 393 U.S. at 511 (quoting Burnside v. Byars, 363 F.2d 744, 749 [CA5 1966]).

In sum, just as access to ideas makes it possible for citizens generally to exercise their rights of free speech and press in a meaningful manner, such access prepares students for active and effective participation in the pluralistic, often contentious society in which they will soon be adult members. Of course all First Amendment rights accorded to students must be construed "in light of the special characteristics of the school environment." *Tinker* v. *Des Moines School Dist.*, 393 U.S. at 506. But the special characteristics of the school library make that environment especially appropriate for the recognition of the First Amendment rights of students.

A school library, no less than any other public library, is "a place dedicated to quiet, to knowledge, and to beauty." *Brown* v. *Louisiana*, 383 U.S. 131, 142 (1966) (opinion of Fortas, J.). *Keyishian* v. *Board of Regents*, 385 U.S. 589 (1967), observed that "students must always remain free to inquire, to study and to evaluate, to gain new maturity and understanding." The school library is the principal locus of such freedom. As one District Court has well put it, in the school library,

> a student can literally explore the unknown, and discover areas of interest and thought not covered by the prescribed curriculum. . . . Th[e] student learns that a library is a place to test or expand upon ideas presented to him, in or out of the classroom. *Right to Read Defense Committee* v. *School Committee*, 454 F.Supp. 703, 715 (Mass.1978).

Petitioners emphasize the inculcative function of secondary education, and argue that they must be allowed unfettered discretion to "transmit community values" through the Island Trees schools. But that sweeping claim overlooks the unique role of the school library. It appears from the record that use of the Island Trees school libraries is completely voluntary on the part of students. Their selection of books from these libraries is entirely a matter of free choice; the libraries afford them an opportunity at self-education and individual enrichment that is wholly optional. Petitioners might well defend their claim of absolute discretion in matters of curriculum by reliance upon their duty to inculcate community values. But we think that petitioners' reliance upon that duty is misplaced where, as here, they attempt to extend their claim of absolute discretion beyond the compulsory environment of the classroom, into the school library and the regime of voluntary inquiry that there holds sway.

(2)

In rejecting petitioners' claim of absolute discretion to remove books from their school libraries, we do not deny that local school boards have a substantial legitimate role to play in the determination of school library content. We thus must turn to the question of the extent to which the First Amendment places limitations upon the discretion of petitioners to remove books from their libraries. In this inquiry, we enjoy the guidance of several precedents. *West Virginia Board of Education* v. *Barnette* stated:

> If there is any fixed star in our constitutional constellation, it is that no official, high or petty, can prescribe what shall be orthodox in politics, nationalism, religion, or other matters of opinion. . . . If there are any circumstances which permit an exception, they do not now occur to us. 319 U.S. at 642.

This doctrine has been reaffirmed in later cases involving education. For example, *Keyishian* v. *Board of Regents*, supra, at 603, noted that "the First Amendment . . . does not tolerate laws that cast a pall of orthodoxy over the classroom;" see also *Epperson* v. *Arkansas*, 393 U.S. at 104–105. And *Mt. Healthy City Board of Ed.* v. *Doyle*, 429 U.S. 274 (1977), recognized First Amendment limitations upon the discretion of a local school board to refuse to rehire a nontenured teacher. The school board in *Mt. Healthy* had declined to renew respondent Doyle's employment contract, in part because he had exercised his First Amendment rights. Although Doyle did not have tenure, and thus "could have been discharged for no reason whatever," *Mt. Healthy* held that he could "nonetheless establish a claim to reinstatement if the decision not to rehire him was made by reason of his exercise of constitutionally protected First Amendment freedoms." *Id.* at 283–284. We held further that once Doyle had shown that his conduct was constitutionally protected, and that this conduct was a 'substantial factor' . . . in the Board's decision not to rehire him," the school board was obliged to show "by a preponderance of the evidence that it would have reached the same decision as to respondent's reemployment even in the absence of the protected conduct." *Id.* at 287.

With respect to the present case, the message of these precedents is clear. Petitioners rightly possess significant discretion to determine the content of their school libraries. But that discretion may not be exercised in a narrowly partisan or political manner. If a Democratic school board, motivated by party affiliation, ordered the removal of all books written by or in favor of Republicans, few would doubt that the order violated the constitutional rights of the students denied access to those books. The same conclusion would surely apply if an all-white school board, motivated by racial animus, decided to remove all books authored by blacks or advocating racial equality and integration. Our Constitution does not permit the official suppression of *ideas*. Thus, whether petitioners' removal of books from their school libraries denied respondents their First Amendment rights depends upon the motivation behind petitioners' actions. If petitioners *intended* by their removal decision to deny respondents access to ideas with which petitioners disagreed, and if this intent was the decisive factor in petitioners' decision, then petitioners have exercised their discretion in violation of the Constitution. To permit such intentions to control official actions would be to encourage the precise sort of officially prescribed orthodoxy unequivocally condemned in *Barnette*. On the other hand, respondents implicitly concede that an unconstitutional motivation would *not* be demonstrated if it were shown that petitioners had decided to remove the books at issue because those books were pervasively vulgar. Tr. of Oral Arg. 36. And again, respondents concede that, if it were demonstrated that the removal decision was based solely upon the "educational suitability" of the books in question, then their removal would be "perfectly permissible." *Id*. at 53. In other words, in respondents' view, such motivations, if decisive of petitioners' actions, would not carry the danger of an official suppression of ideas, and thus would not violate respondents' First Amendment rights.

As noted earlier, nothing in our decision today affects in any way the discretion of a local school board to choose books to *add* to the libraries of their schools. Because we are concerned in this case with the suppression of ideas, our holding today affects only the discretion to *remove* books. In brief, we hold that local school boards may not remove books from school library shelves simply because they dislike the ideas contained in those books and seek by their removal to "prescribe what shall be orthodox in politics, nationalism, religion, or other matters of opinion." *West Virginia Board of Education* v. *Barnette*, 319 U.S. at 642. Such purposes stand inescapably condemned by our precedents.

B

We now turn to the remaining question presented by this case: do the evidentiary materials that were before the District Court, when construed most favorably to respondents, raise a genuine issue of material fact whether petitioners exceeded constitutional limitations in exercising their discretion to remove the books from the school libraries? We conclude that the materials do raise such a question, which foreclose summary judgment in favor of petitioners.

Before the District Court, respondents claimed that petitioners' decision to remove the books "was based on [their] personal values, morals and tastes." App. 139. Respondents also claimed that petitioners objected to the books in part because excerpts from them were "anti-American." *Id.* at 140. The accuracy of these claims was partially conceded by petitioner and petitioners' own affidavits lent further support to respondents' claims. In addition, the record developed in the District Court shows that, when petitioners offered their first public explanation for the removal of the books, they relied in part on the assertion that the removed books were "anti-American," and "offensive to . . . Americans in general." 474 F.Supp. at 390. Furthermore, while the Book Review Committee appointed by petitioners was instructed to make its recommendations based upon criteria that appear on their face to be permissible—the books' "educational suitability," "good taste," "relevance," and "appropriateness to age and grade level," App. 67—the Committee's recommendations that five of the books be retained and that only two be removed were essentially rejected by petitioners, without any statement of reasons for doing so. Finally, while petitioners originally defended their removal decision with the explanation that "these books contain obscenities, blasphemies, brutality, and perversion beyond description," 474 F.Supp. at 390, one of the books, *A Reader for Writers,* was removed even though it contained no such language. 638 F.2d at 428, n. 6 (Mansfield, J., dissenting).

Standing alone, this evidence respecting the substantive motivations behind petitioners' removal decision would not be decisive. This would be a very different case if the record demonstrated that petitioners had employed established, regular, and facially unbiased procedures for the review of controversial materials. But the actual record in the case before us suggests the exact opposite. Petitioners' removal procedures were vigorously challenged below by respondents, and the evidence on this issue sheds further light on the issue of petitioners' motivations. Respondents alleged that, in making their removal decision petitioners ignored "the advice of literary experts," the views of "librarians and teachers within the Island Trees School system," the advice of the Superintendent of Schools, and the guidance of publications that rate books for junior and senior high school students. App. 128–129. Respondents also claimed that petitioners' decision was based solely on the fact that the books were named on the PONYU list received by petitioners Ahrens, Martin, and Hughes, and that petitioners "did not undertake an independent review of other books in the [school] libraries." *Id*. at 129–130. Evidence before the District Court lends support to these claims. The record shows that, immediately after petitioners first ordered the books removed from the library shelves, the Superintendent of Schools reminded them that "we already have a policy . . . designed expressly to handle such problems," and recommended that the removal decision be approached through this established channel. See n.4, *supra*. But the Board disregarded the Superintendent's advice, and instead resorted to the extraordinary procedure of appointing a Book Review Committee—the advice of which was later rejected without explanation. In sum, respondents' allegations and some of the evidentiary materials presented below do not rule out the possibility that petitioners' removal procedures were highly irregular and ad hoc—the antithesis of those procedures that might tend to allay suspicions regarding petitioners' motivations.

Construing these claims, affidavit statements, and other evidentiary materials in a manner favorable to respondents, we cannot conclude that petitioners were "entitled to a judgment as a matter of law." The evidence plainly does not foreclose the possibility that petitioners' decision to remove the books rested decisively upon disagreement with constitutionally protected ideas in those books, or upon a desire on petitioners' part to impose upon the students of the Island Trees High School and Junior High School a political orthodoxy to which petitioners and their constituents adhered. Of course, some of the evidence before the District Court might lead a finder of fact to accept petitioners' claim that their removal decision was based upon constitutionally valid concerns. But that evidence, at most, creates a genuine issue of material fact on the critical question of the credibility of petitioners' justifications for their decision: On that issue, it simply cannot be said that there is no genuine issue as to any material fact.

The mandate shall issue forthwith.

Affirmed.

Appendix B

U.S. FREEDOM OF INFORMATION ACT (**5 U.S.C.** SEC. **552**)

(a) Each agency shall make available to the public information as follows:

  (1) Each agency shall separately state and currently publish in the Federal Register for the guidance of the public—

    (A) descriptions of its central and field organization and the established places at which, the employees (and in the case of a uniformed service, the members) from whom, and the methods whereby, the public may obtain information, make submittals or requests, or obtain decisions;

    (B) statements of the general course and method by which its functions are channeled and determined, including the nature and requirements of all formal and informal procedures available;

    (C) rules of procedure, descriptions of forms available or the places at which forms may be obtained, and instructions as to the scope and contents of all papers, reports, or examinations;

    (D) substantive rules of general applicability adopted as authorized by law, and statements of general policy or interpretations of general applicability formulated and adopted by the agency; and

    (E) each amendment, revision, or repeal of the foregoing. Except to the extent that a person has actual and timely notice of the terms thereof, a person may not in any manner be required to resort to, or be adversely affected by, a matter required to be published in the Federal Register and not so published. For the purpose of this paragraph, matter reasonably available to the class of persons affected thereby is deemed published in the Federal Register when incorporated by reference therein with the approval of the Director of the Federal Register.

(2) Each agency, in accordance with published rules, shall make available for public inspection and copying—

(A) final opinions, including concurring and dissenting opinions, as well as orders, made in the adjudication of cases;

(B) those statements of policy and interpretations which have been adopted by the agency and are not published in the Federal Register; and

(C) administrative staff manuals and instructions to staff that affect a member of the public; unless the materials are promptly published and copies offered for sale. To the extent required to prevent a clearly unwarranted invasion of personal privacy, an agency may delete identifying details when it makes available or publishes an opinion, statement of policy, interpretation, or staff manual or instruction. However, in each case the justification for the deletion shall be explained fully in writing. Each agency shall also maintain and make available for public inspection and copying current indexes providing identifying information for the public as to any matter issued, adopted, or promulgated after July 4, 1967, and required by this paragraph to be made available or published. Each agency shall promptly publish, quarterly or more frequently, and distribute (by sale or otherwise) copies of each index or supplements thereto unless it determines by order published in the Federal Register that the publication would be unnecessary and impracticable, in which case the agency shall nonetheless provide copies of such index on request at a cost not to exceed the direct cost of duplication. A final order, opinion, statement of policy, interpretation, or staff manual or instruction that affects a member of the public may be relied on, used, or cited as precedent by an agency against a party other than an agency only if—

(i)   it has been indexed and either made available or published as provided by this paragraph; or

(ii) the party has actual and timely notice of the terms thereof.

(3) Except with respect to the records made available under

paragraphs (1) and (2) of this subsection, each agency, upon any request for records which

(A) reasonably describes such records and

(B) is made in accordance with published rules stating the time, place, fees (if any), and procedures to be followed, shall make the records promptly available to any person.

(4) (A) (i) In order to carry out the provisions of this section, each agency shall promulgate regulations, pursuant to notice and receipt of public comment, specifying the schedule of fees applicable to the processing of requests under this section and establishing procedures and guidelines for determining when such fees should be waived or reduced. Such schedule shall conform to the guidelines which shall be promulgated, pursuant to notice and receipt of public comment, by the Director of the Office of Management and Budget and which shall provide for a uniform schedule of fees for all agencies.

(ii) Such agency regulations shall provide that—

(I) fees shall be limited to reasonable standard charges for document search, duplication, and review, when records are requested for commercial use;

(II) fees shall be limited to reasonable standard charges for document duplication when records are not sought for commercial use and the request is made by an educational or noncommercial scientific institution, whose purpose is scholarly or scientific research; or a representative of the news media; and

(III) for any request not described in (I) or (II), fees shall be limited to reasonable standard charges for document search and duplication.

(iii) Documents shall be furnished without any charge or at a charge reduced below the fees established under clause (ii) if disclosure of the information is in the public interest because it is likely to contribute significantly to public understanding of the operations or activities of the government and is not primarily in the commercial interest of the requester.

(iv) Fee schedules shall provide for the recovery of only the direct costs of search, duplication, or review. Review costs shall include only the direct costs incurred during the initial examination of a document for the purposes of determining whether the documents must be disclosed under this section and for the purposes of withholding any portions exempt from disclosure under this section. Review costs may not include any costs incurred in resolving issues of law or policy that may be raised in the course of processing a request under this section. No fee may be charged by any agency under this section—

    (I)   if the costs of routine collection and processing of the fee are likely to equal or exceed the amount of the fee; or

    (II) for any request described in clause (ii) (II) or (III) of this subparagraph for the first two hours of search time or for the first one hundred pages of duplication.

(v) No agency may require advance payment of any fee unless the requester has previously failed to pay fees in a timely fashion, or the agency has determined that the fee will exceed $250.

(vi) Nothing in this subparagraph shall supersede fees chargeable under a statute specifically providing for setting the level of fees for particular types of records.

(vii) In any action by a requester regarding the waiver of fees under this section, the court shall determine the matter de novo: Provided, That the court's review of the matter shall be limited to the record before the agency.

(B) On complaint, the district court of the United States in the district in which the complainant resides, or has his principal place of business, or in which the agency records are situated, or in the District of Columbia, has jurisdiction to enjoin the agency from withholding agency records and to order the production of any agency records improperly withheld from the complainant. In such a case the court shall determine the matter de novo, and may examine the contents of such agency records in camera to determine whether such records or any part thereof shall be withheld under any of the exemptions set forth in subsection (b) of this section, and the burden is on the agency to sustain its action.

(C) Notwithstanding any other provision of law, the defendant shall serve an answer or otherwise plead to any complaint made under this subsection within thirty days after service upon the defendant of the pleading in which such complaint is made, unless the court otherwise directs for good cause shown.

(D) Repealed. Pub. L. 98-620, title IV, Sec. 402(2), Nov. 8, 1984, 98 Stat. 3357.

(E) The court may assess against the United States reasonable attorney fees and other litigation costs reasonably incurred in any case under this section in which the complainant has substantially prevailed.

(F) Whenever the court orders the production of any agency records improperly withheld from the complainant and assesses against the United States reasonable attorney fees and other litigation costs, and the court additionally issues a written finding that the circumstances surrounding the withholding raise questions whether agency personnel acted arbitrarily or capriciously with respect to the withholding, the Special Counsel shall promptly initiate a proceeding to determine whether disciplinary action is warranted against the officer or employee who was primarily responsible for the withholding. The Special Counsel, after investigation and consideration of the evidence submitted, shall submit his findings and recommendations to the administrative authority of the agency concerned and shall send copies of the findings and recommendations to the officer or employee or his representative. The administrative authority shall take the corrective action that the Special Counsel recommends.

(G) In the event of noncompliance with the order of the court, the district court may punish for contempt the responsible employee, and in the case of a uniformed service, the responsible member.

(5) Each agency having more than one member shall maintain and make available for public inspection a record of the final votes of each member in every agency proceeding.

(6) (A) Each agency, upon any request for records made under paragraph (1), (2), or (3) of this subsection, shall—

    (i)   determine within ten days (excepting Saturdays, Sundays, and legal public holidays) after the receipt of any such request whether to comply with such request and shall immediately notify the person making such request of such determination and the reasons therefor, and of the right of such person to appeal to the head of the agency any adverse determination; and

(ii) make a determination with respect to any appeal within twenty days (excepting Saturdays, Sundays, and legal public holidays) after the receipt of such appeal. If on appeal the denial of the request for records is in whole or in part upheld, the agency shall notify the person making such request of the provisions for judicial review of that determination under paragraph (4) of this subsection.

(B) In unusual circumstances as specified in this subparagraph, the time limits prescribed in either clause (i) or clause (ii) of subparagraph (A) may be extended by written notice to the person making such request setting forth the reasons for such extension and the date on which a determination is expected to be dispatched. No such notice shall specify a date that would result in an extension for more than ten working days. As used in this subparagraph, 'unusual circumstances' means, but only to the extent reasonably necessary to the proper processing of the particular request—

(i)   the need to search for and collect the requested records from field facilities or other establishments that are separate from the office processing the request;

(ii) the need to search for, collect, and appropriately examine a voluminous amount of separate and distinct records which are demanded in a single request; or

(iii) the need for consultation, which shall be conducted with all practicable speed, with another agency having a substantial interest in the determination of the request or among two or more components of the agency having substantial subject-matter interest therein.

(C) Any person making a request to any agency for records under paragraph (1), (2), or (3) of this subsection shall be deemed to have exhausted his administrative remedies with respect to such request if the agency fails to comply with the applicable time limit provisions of this paragraph. If the Government can show exceptional circumstances exist and that the agency is exercising due diligence in responding to the request, the court may retain jurisdiction and allow the agency additional time to complete its review of the records. Upon any determination by an agency to comply with a request for records, the records shall be made promptly available to such person making such request. Any notification of denial of any request for records under this subsection shall set forth the names and titles or positions of each person responsible for the denial of such request.

(b) This section does not apply to matters that are—

(1) (A) specifically authorized under criteria established by an Executive order to be kept secret in the interest of national defense or foreign policy and

(B) are in fact properly classified pursuant to such Executive order;

(2) related solely to the internal personnel rules and practices of an agency;

(3) specifically exempted from disclosure by statute (other than section 552b of this title), provided that such statute

(A) requires that the matters be withheld from the public in such a manner as to leave no discretion on the issue, or

(B) establishes particular criteria for withholding or refers to particular types of matters to be withheld;

(4) trade secrets and commercial or financial information obtained from a person and privileged or confidential;

(5) inter-agency or intra-agency memorandums or letters which would not be available by law to a party other than an agency in litigation with the agency;

(6) personnel and medical files and similar files the disclosure of which would constitute a clearly unwarranted invasion of personal privacy;

(7) records or information compiled for law enforcement purposes, but only to the extent that the production of such law enforcement records or information

(A) could reasonably be expected to interfere with enforcement proceedings,

(B) would deprive a person of a right to a fair trial or an impartial adjudication,

(C) could reasonably be expected to constitute an unwarranted invasion of personal privacy,

(D) could reasonably be expected to disclose the identity of a confidential source, including a State, local, or foreign agency or authority or any private institution which furnished information on a confidential basis, and, in the case of a record or information compiled by criminal law enforcement authority in the course of a criminal investigation or by an agency conducting a lawful national security intelligence investigation, information furnished by a confidential source,

(E) would disclose techniques and procedures for law enforcement investigations or prosecutions, or would disclose guidelines for law enforcement investigations or prosecutions if such disclosure could reasonably be expected to risk circumvention of the law, or

(F) could reasonably be expected to endanger the life or physical safety of any individual;

(8) contained in or related to examination, operating, or condition reports prepared by, on behalf of, or for the use of an agency responsible for the regulation or supervision of financial institutions; or

(9) geological and geophysical information and data, including maps, concerning wells.

Any reasonably segregable portion of a record shall be provided to any person requesting such record after deletion of the portions which are exempt under this subsection.

(c) (1) Whenever a request is made which involves access to records described in subsection (b)(7)(A) and—

(A) the investigation or proceeding involves a possible violation of criminal law; and

(B) there is reason to believe that

(i)   the subject of the investigation or proceeding is not aware of its pendency, and

(ii) disclosure of the existence of the records could reasonably be expected to interfere with enforcement proceedings, the agency may, during only such time as that circumstance continues, treat the records as not subject to the requirements of this section.

(2) Whenever informant records maintained by a criminal law enforcement agency under an informant's name or personal identifier are requested by a third party according to the informant's name or personal identifier, the agency may treat the records as not subject to the requirements of this section unless the informant's status as an informant has been officially confirmed.

(3) Whenever a request is made which involves access to records maintained by the Federal Bureau of Investigation pertaining to foreign intelligence or counterintelligence, or

international terrorism, and the existence of the records is classified information as provided in subsection (b)(1), the Bureau may, as long as the existence of the records remains classified information, treat the records as not subject to the requirements of this section.

(d) This section does not authorize withholding of information or limit the availability of records to the public, except as specifically stated in this section. This section is not authority to withhold information from Congress.

(e) On or before March 1 of each calendar year, each agency shall submit a report covering the preceding calendar year to the Speaker of the House of Representatives and President of the Senate for referral to the appropriate committees of the Congress. The report shall include—

(1) the number of determinations made by such agency not to comply with requests for records made to such agency under subsection (a) and the reasons for each such determination;

(2) the number of appeals made by persons under subsection (a)(6), the result of such appeals, and the reason for the action upon each appeal that results in a denial of information;

(3) the names and titles or positions of each person responsible for the denial of records requested under this section, and the number of instances of participation for each;

(4) the results of each proceeding conducted pursuant to subsection (a)(4)(F), including a report of the disciplinary action taken against the officer or employee who was primarily responsible for improperly withholding records or an explanation of why disciplinary action was not taken; (5) a copy of every rule made by such agency regarding this section;

(6) a copy of the fee schedule and the total amount of fees collected by the agency for making records available under this section; and

(7) such other information as indicates efforts to administer fully this section.

The Attorney General shall submit an annual report on or before March 1 of each calendar year which shall include for the prior calendar year a listing of the number of cases arising under this section, the exemption involved in each case, the disposition of such case, and the cost, fees, and penalties assessed under subsections (a)(4)(E), (F), and (G). Such report shall also include a description of the efforts undertaken by the Department of Justice to encourage agency compliance with this section.

(f) For purposes of this section, the term 'agency' as defined in section 551(1) of this title includes any executive department, military department, Government corporation, Government controlled corporation, or other establishment in the executive branch of the Government (including the Executive Office of the President), or any independent regulatory agency.

SHORT TITLE: This section is popularly known as the 'Freedom of Information Act'.

Index

KF
4315
B54
1995

Bielefield, Arlene.

Library patrons and the law.

$35.00

DATE			

KF
4315
B54

CARROLL COMMUNITY COLLEGE LMTS

Library patrons and the law.

00000009248717

Library / Media Center
Carroll Community College
1601 Washington Road
Westminster, Maryland

WITHDRAWN

1996

BAKER & TAYLOR